GROW
ALL YOU CAN EAT IN
3 SQUARE FEET

GROW
ALL YOU CAN EAT IN
3 SQUARE FEET

Horticultural Consultant Naomi Schillinger
Senior Editor Chauney Dunford
Senior Art Editor Clare Marshall
Editor Tia Sarkar
Illustrator Bryony Fripp
Senior Jacket Creative Nicola Powling
Jacket Designer Ria Holland
Senior Producer Che Creasey
Preproduction Producer Andy Hilliard
Managing Editor Penny Warren
Publisher Mary Ling
Art Director Jane Bull

DK Publishing
US Editor Kate Johnsen
US Consultant Lori Spencer
US Senior Editor Shannon Beatty

First American Edition, 2015
Published in the United States by
DK Publishing, 345 Hudson Street
New York, New York 10014
15 16 17 18 10 9 8 7 6 5 4 3 2

005–195596–February/2015

DK books are available at special discounts when
purchased in bulk for sales promotions, premiums,
fund-raising, or educational use. For details,
contact: DK Publishing Special Markets, 345
Hudson Street, New York, New York 10014 or
SpecialSales@dk.com.

Published in Great Britain by
Dorling Kindersley Limited.

A catalog record for this book is available from the
Library of Congress.

ISBN 978-1-4654-2980-3

DK books are available at special discounts when
purchased in bulk for sales promotions, premiums,
fund-raising, or educational use. For details,
contact: DK Publishing Special Markets, 345
Hudson Street, New York, New York 10014 or
SpecialSales@dk.com.
Printed and bound by Leo Paper
Products Ltd, China.

www.dk.com

Contents

MAKING A START

3 golden rules for growing your own crops

1

GET TO KNOW YOUR PLOT

● Identify every space in your yard where you could grow crops, including in pots, and ensure these areas are suitable for plants (*see pp.14–19*).

2

DECIDE WHAT YOU WANT TO GROW

● Consider the crops you'd like to grow, and work out if you have the space (*see pp.32–33*) and can give them the right conditions (*see pp.224–241*).

3

MAXIMIZING YOUR HARVEST

● Make the most of the space and time you have. Start your plants early, keep them healthy, harvest promptly, and resow bare spaces (*see pp.42–57*).

Where can I grow crops?

...practically anywhere.

In the soil

If you have space, the **best place** to grow your crops is directly **in the soil.** Choose the best spot possible (*see pp.14–19*), and **make a bed** as large as you need. Get to **know your soil** and **improve it** if you need to (*see pp.18–19*).

Raised beds

Raised beds are a **great option** even if you can **plant directly** in the soil, and they have many **advantages** (*see pp.20–21*). They are also **ideal for spaces** where there is **no soil**, such as on a **patio**, or where the **soil is poor**.

Containers

Most crops can be **grown in pots** as long as they are **large enough** for what you want to grow. Containers are a **great option** for smaller yards, and they can also **help you** to make **full use** of every space in even **larger gardens**.

Be creative!

By being creative with the **space** you have and **how you use** it, you'll **be surprised** by the amount of crops **you can grow**. Line your **paths** with pots, hang grow bags over your **balcony**, and **fix shelves** for planting troughs.

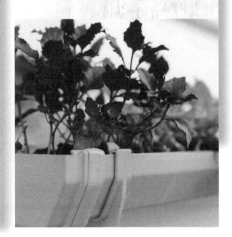

Growing crops in urban areas

What most urban gardens **may lack in size**, they make up for with **opportunities**. Being able to grow **fresh fruit and vegetables** within sight of your home is **highly rewarding**, and also surprisingly **straightforward**.

Light

- Closely packed buildings create pockets of light and shade, of which you can take advantage.
- Prune back any overhanging branches of larger trees and shrubs to allow more light into your garden.
- Walls overlooking your garden could be painted white to reflect extra light onto your crops.

Temperature

- Urban gardens are sheltered and warmed by surrounding buildings, creating mild "urban heat islands."
- The sheltered conditions allow an earlier start in spring and a long growing season.
- The mild temperatures allow you to grow tender crops, such as cucumbers.

Water

- Crops growing in containers will need frequent watering. Consider installing a water barrel or an outside tap.
- Walls and fences can prevent the rain from reaching your plants, so check them regularly to see if they need watering.

Wind

- Balconies and rooftop gardens can be exposed to wind, so choose low-growing crops and support taller plants.
- Nearby buildings can channel the wind, so install windbreaks, such as trellis or wind-resistant plants.
- When positioning pots on shelves or putting up hanging baskets, ensure they cannot be blown off.

5 benefits of urban gardens

- They tend to be warmer in winter, ideal for tender crops.

- They warm up quickly in spring, giving your crops an earlier start.

- The shelter from nearby buildings encourages rapid plant growth.

- An early start and a late finish gives your crops a long growing season.

- Often smaller, they are easy to maintain.

Weighty issues

- If you garden on a balcony or roof terrace, be careful not to overload it. Wet compost is very heavy, and your growing plants will gain weight.
- When putting up wall shelves and brackets for containers and baskets, be sure they are firmly attached and will safely take the necessary weight.

Understanding light

The amount of light in your garden plays an important role when planning what to grow. Some crops, such as tomatoes and chili peppers, need at least six hours of sun a day to grow well, while lettuce thrives in just three.

The longest summer's day in the US provides nearly 16 hours of daylight. In Fairbanks, AK, the shortest winter's day has less than 4 hours of light.

The effects of light and shade

Full sun

- Sunny sites can be very **warm**, and plants need watering often.
- **Fruit**, such as tomatoes, **ripen** more quickly in full sun.
- Most plants **flower** more **readily** in full sun, which is essential for **fruiting** crops.
- Heat can **stress** crops, leaving them prone to **disease**. Leaf crops may "bolt" (suddenly flower).

Partial sun

- East- and west-facing plots offer **a balance** of sun and shade, and suit **many crops**.
- Many **sun-loving** crops can be grown in partial sun, although **won't crop** as freely.
- You may be able to **reduce** the amount of shade in your garden by removing **shadow-forming** plants and structures.

Partial shade

- Shady plots are **colder** and are slow to warm up in **spring**.
- Sun-loving plants grow **weak and spindly** when grown in shade.
- Most **leafy crops** prefer some shade; they can **scorch** if positioned in full sun.
- **Slugs and snails** prefer cool, damp areas, and can be a **problem** in shadier gardens.

Make a photo diary

Grab your **camera** and start noting where **sun and shade** occur in your garden **throughout** the day. This will help you to find the **brightest** spots for your crops.

10AM

12 NOON

3PM

5PM

What does full sun actually mean?

Urban gardens often only have sun for part of the day. So in these conditions, full sun means direct sunlight for at least six hours a day, and for shadier areas, a minimum of three hours a day.

SUMMER Light levels are good at this time because the sun is at its highest in the sky, at least until midsummer. There is less shadow, and the days are warmer and longer, which encourages plant growth.

WINTER Light levels are poor because the sun is low in the sky and the light itself is less intense. The days are also cool and short, especially in northern areas, meaning that plant growth is very slow.

Water

Water is vital for healthy crops, and since growing them in small spaces often means doing so in containers, you need to be prepared to water them often. Taking these steps will make this easier.

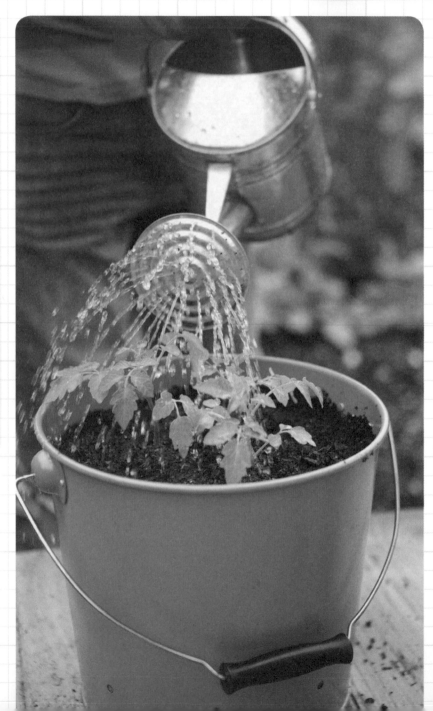

- Use **larger pots**, since these dry out **less quickly**.
- Stand your pots on **drip trays** to keep the soil mix moist.
- **Soak plants** well before planting to encourage **rooting**.
- Be aware of the **rain shadows** around your garden.

Easier watering

To make watering easier, add an outside tap, or site a water barrel near your crops. Buy a hose that will reach your plants easily and a good reel to store it neatly. Micro-irrigation kits and seep hoses can save hours of time and are easy to implement. Also, mulch your pots to prevent evaporation.

Exposure

Being exposed to strong wind causes plants to dry out more quickly and can scorch the leaves and damage the stems. Balconies and roof gardens are most at risk, although any area can be affected if nearby buildings create wind tunnels. Wind can be defeated, however.

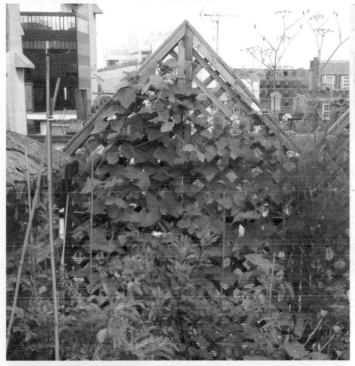

- Use trellises to **filter and slow** the wind, so it is less damaging. A trellis also offers **support to climbers**.
- Avoid solid windbreaks that cause **damaging currents** on the opposite side.
- Position new **greenhouses and sheds** to break up wind tunnels affecting your plot.
- Use **multilayered** barriers of plants and structures to **diffuse strong winds**.
- Add low-level barriers, **like netting** or sheets of plastic, to help **low-growing** crops.
- Use **cloches** to help protect vulnerable **young plants**.

Windproof plants

Tougher plants that withstand and filter the wind can make an attractive feature, and can also be used to provide habitat for beneficial wildlife. Try wild roses (*Rosa*), hawthorn (*Crataegus*), and shrubby honeysuckles (*Lonicera*). Grasses also work well, swaying in the breeze.

Closer to the ground, use Mediterranean plants, such as lavender (*Lavandula*) and sage (*Salvia*). Grow them at the edges of beds to protect your leafy crops from wind scorch.

Getting to know your soil

Whether you grow them in pots or directly in borders or raised beds, healthy plants that crop well rely on healthy soil, which makes them more resistant to pests and diseases. By getting to know your soil, you will understand how to improve it to get the best results.

- The **ideal soil**, such as **loam** (*see right*), retains **moisture** and **nutrients** well, but drains freely.
- **Most** garden soils are rich in either **heavy clay** or **sand**.
- All soil types can be improved by adding **organic matter** to increase **drainage**, or moisture and nutrient **retention**.

Loam
This is the perfect garden soil, comprising a well-balanced mixture of clay, sand, and silt particles, and organic matter.

Clay soil
Heavy clay soil holds onto nutrients well, but drains poorly. It can be heavy to dig when wet and can bake hard in summer.

Sandy soil
Light sandy soil drains very freely, leaching moisture and nutrients. It is always worth improving it with organic matter.

Checking your soil type

Your soil type can be easily tested just by rubbing a small amount between your fingers. Clay soil, with its sticky texture, will be easy to mold into balls that will hold their shape. Sandy soils will feel gritty to the touch and won't hold together; loamy soils will feel silky and should mold into shapes fairly well.

Is your soil acidic or alkaline?

The pH of your soil will influence the crops you can grow, and it can be easily tested using a kit bought from a garden center. Most vegetables prefer slightly acidic soil, and although soil pH can be altered, it's best to grow the crops that suit the soil you have. If your soil isn't ideal for what you want to grow, plant in pots or in a raised bed instead.

Improving your soil

Well-rotted organic matter is ideal for improving both clay and sandy soils. Rather than digging it in, however, lay it on the surface as a mulch, and allow earthworms to draw it into the soil. As they tunnel and feed, worms aerate the soil and improve its structure.

Clay soil

Clay soil is made up of very fine particles that stick together, which impedes drainage. Adding coarse organic matter physically breaks up the clay, making it lighter to dig and improving drainage.

Recycled green waste

Garden or park waste is often available from recycling centers and local municipal authorities. This nutrient-rich compost will aerate the soil and act as a slow-release feed.

Well-rotted manure

Manure is full of degraded straw, which helps break up clay soil. It is also rich in nutrients and acts as a slow-release feed. Only use well-rotted manure, never fresh.

Sandy soil

Sandy soil is very porous, meaning that moisture and soluble nutrients are quickly lost. Adding bulky organic matter works like a sponge, helping to retain moisture and nutrients in the soil for longer.

Homemade garden compost

Absolutely free, it acts as a slow-release fertilizer, and improves the aeration and water retention of your soil. It can also be used to fill containers if mixed with soil.

Leaf mold

This is excellent for increasing the water retention and organic content of light soils. It's easy to make: store wet fall leaves in bags for two years, and it's ready to use.

Making your own garden compost

Any disease-free leafy and twiggy plant material can be added to a compost heap, which breaks down over a few months to produce a good all-around soil improver—all for free.

Adding plant material
To fill a compost bin, add leafy and twiggy material and kitchen waste in layers. Doing this will ensure good airflow.

Turning the compost bin
Continue adding material and periodically turn the heap using a fork. This adds air and encourages the composting process.

The finished compost
Compost is ready to use when it is dark and crumbly. Empty the compost out and return material that isn't decomposed to the bin.

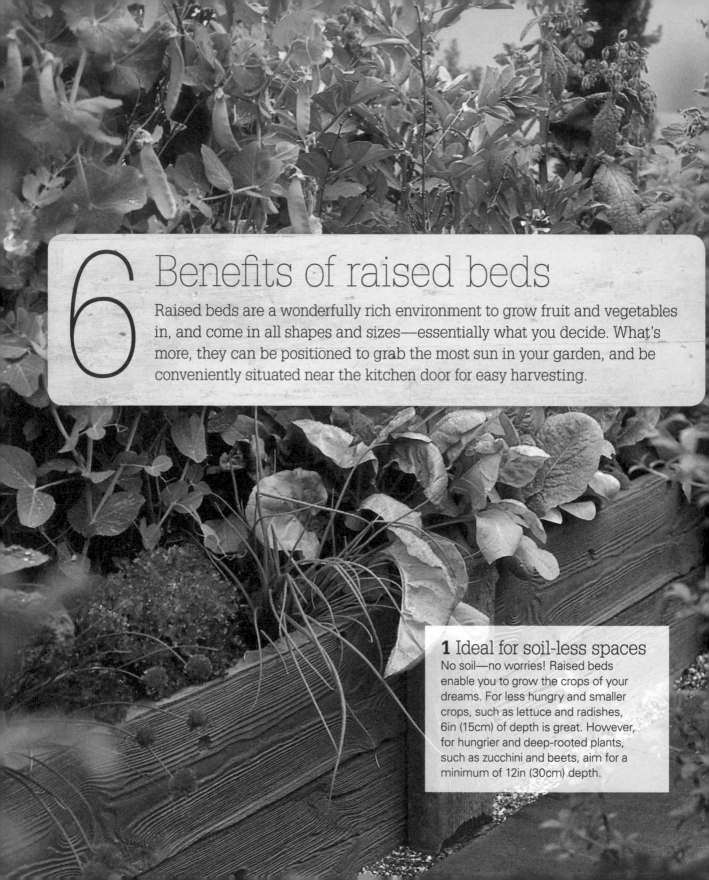

6 Benefits of raised beds

Raised beds are a wonderfully rich environment to grow fruit and vegetables in, and come in all shapes and sizes—essentially what you decide. What's more, they can be positioned to grab the most sun in your garden, and be conveniently situated near the kitchen door for easy harvesting.

1 Ideal for soil-less spaces

No soil—no worries! Raised beds enable you to grow the crops of your dreams. For less hungry and smaller crops, such as lettuce and radishes, 6in (15cm) of depth is great. However, for hungrier and deep-rooted plants, such as zucchini and beets, aim for a minimum of 12in (30cm) depth.

2 Providing ideal growing conditions

Many gardens have problematic soil, whether heavy clay or very light and sandy. Building raised beds, and adding the perfect blend of soil mix and topsoil (*see pp.22–23*), will allow you to instantly start growing a whole range of exciting fruit, herbs, and vegetables.

3 Temporary growing space

If you rent your home, have building plans on the horizon, or are dabbling in a bit of guerrilla gardening on a patch of unloved public space (and why not?), raised beds are ideal. They are quick, cheap, and easy to construct, and they allow you to quickly start growing, even if it's just for one season.

4 Using recycled materials

The world is your oyster when it comes to using recycled materials to make raised beds. Old bricks, scaffolding boards, and metal sheets are ideal materials. Or, plant directly into used tires or even an old wading pool.

5 Protecting crops from pests

Compared to traditional vegetable patches, raised beds, being contained areas, are much easier to protect against pests. Netting can be secured along the sides to keep birds from stealing your succulent fruit or to prevent butterflies from laying eggs on your brassica crops. Use chicken wire to deter larger pests, such as birds, cats, foxes, and deer.

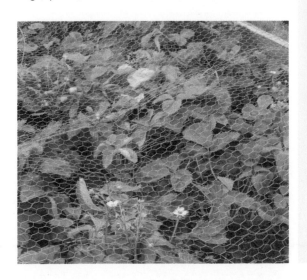

6 Giving you easier access

Making your beds no wider than 3–4ft (1–1.2m) across will make it easier for you to tend your crops without the need to tread on the soil, compacting it. The higher the bed, the less bending down you'll have to do, which can be a godsend if you have a bad back or troublesome knees.

An early start

A **useful advantage** of raised beds is that they **warm up** more **quickly** in spring. This allows you to **sow and plant** out **earlier** than you could if growing your crops **directly** in the soil. An **early start** gives you **more time** to grow **crops**.

Raised beds are ideal for gardens with no soil, and can easily be sited on decks, roof terraces, and patios. Just be sure that any water that drains from the base has somewhere to go.

The perfect height

To provide adequate depth for plant roots, raised beds should provide at least 6in (15cm) of soil. However, they can be much deeper, even allowing you to grow crops with big tubers, such as potatoes. Deeper beds also have the advantage of retaining moisture better, so are less prone to drying out.

Filling your raised bed

Building a raised bed gives you the perfect opportunity to provide your plants with the ideal growing conditions to ensure the best crops. Using the ratio below, mix the topsoil, soil mix, and coarse grit together in a wheelbarrow or on a large sheet of plastic on the ground before filling the bed.

45% topsoil

45% peat-free soil mix

10% coarse grit

Wondrous worms

Worms are an essential ally in the garden, and are vital to healthy soil. Feeding on organic matter, such as garden compost and rotting leaves, they draw it deeply into the soil, aerating it as they do so. As they feed, worms release nutrients that in turn feed your plants. Crops in raised beds will also benefit from a healthy worm population, so add some to the soil, and encourage them to stay by mulching.

Do you dig it?

The "No Dig" approach is an alternative gardening method. Not turning the soil, and disturbing it as little as possible, maintains the soil's complex structure and prevents weed seeds from being brought to the surface. Rather than turning it over every year, the soil is instead mulched with well-rotted organic matter, such as garden compost. Worms then work the material into the soil.

1 Finding the
best locations
By using pots, you can
site them to suit your
plants, whether that's
basking in the sun or in
the cool shade. You can
also move them as the
season changes to find
the best locations.

5 Reasons to use containers

The advantage of growing crops in containers is that they are highly versatile.
Pots allow you to provide the best conditions for your plants, and with artful
positioning, they help you make best use of your space. Whenever possible,
choose larger containers because these retain water and nutrients better.

3 Planting in grow bags

Grow bags make easy, inexpensive containers. Nutrient-hungry crops, such as climbing beans, zucchini, and potatoes, need deep grow bags with rich soil and plenty of water. Grow bags for tomatoes tend to be shallower, so water them often.

4 Making use of small spaces

Some crops, such as pea shoots and round salad carrots, will grow even in small pots, allowing you to make use of the most confined spaces. With clever design ideas, you can utilize almost any area. Consider using shelves, hanging baskets, and saddlebags (*see pp.66–69*).

2 Creating an attractive feature

Be it a gorgeous series of herb pots, welcoming you home with delicious scents, or quirky recycled containers full of edible flowers, producing food can be highly decorative and creative, too. Have fun designing your space!

5 Keeping your crops close at hand

What's not to love about having your dinner growing in pots right there on your patio? Freshly picked herbs and salad leaves, juicy berries, and homegrown tomatoes—nothing tastes better! You'll also save time shopping at the end of a busy day, and use zero food miles, too.

Being creative with containers

The beauty of containers is that they are so versatile. Whether arranged on the ground, attached to walls, hung, or placed on shelves, they allow you to grow crops nearly anywhere.

Look **around** your yard for areas that **provide enough light** to grow plants, **choose** pots that **will fit**, and start growing. **Larger containers** are best, but **even small** ones can **be used** to grow **certain varieties**.

Tender perennial crops, such as cucamelons and figs, can be grown outside in pots over the summer, then brought indoors for the winter.

Containers in every corner

With a little imagination, and possibly some handiwork, pots help make full use of your space. Don't forget that your planters need to be easily accessible for watering and harvesting, however.

Climbing crops, such as cucumbers and beans, make good use of small spaces, since growth is trained vertically. If well watered and fed, all can be grown in large containers.

Grouping containers together can provide a significant amount of growing space, (*see pp.132–155*). By using attractive planters, you can also create a great feature.

Window boxes are ideal for growing smaller crops, such as lettuce, and those that trail, like strawberries. Choose colorful varieties that look as good as they taste.

Saddlebags are easy to make yourself (*see pp.66–69*), and can be hung over railings, such as on balconies. Make them big enough to fill the space you have available.

Hanging baskets make great use of vertical spaces, and can be attached to walls, fences, and garden structures. They are ideal for trailing plants, like trailing tomatoes.

Using shelves and growing your plants in layers is an excellent use of a small space. They can be permanently attached to walls, or placed on ladders as a temporary solution.

Preparing your containers

Container-grown crops **rely on you** to ensure they have adequate **food** and **water**. Keep them **content** by **preparing** their **pots** well and using the **correct soil mix**.

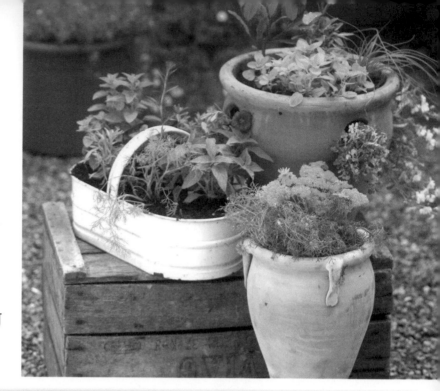

Annual crops
These grow quickly, so require a soil mix that is nutrient rich and retains moisture well.

Use liquid feed for hungry growers, such as tomatoes.

Add slow-release fertilizer to feed crops all season.

Multipurpose potting mix is ideal for vegetables.

MULTIPURPOSE SOIL MIX retains moisture well, and is light and easy to use. However, being made from organic materials, it gradually breaks down over time.

Perennial and shrubby crops
These long-term crops need a soil mix that will support healthy growth for many years.

Slow-release feed can be spread on the surface in spring.

Add sharp grit if your plant needs good drainage.

A heavier soil mix will keep larger plants more stable.

SOIL-BASED POTTING MIX is heavy and keeps potted perennials, shrubs, and trees stable. It doesn't degrade over time and retains nutrients well.

Feeding container plants

Most potting mixes provide enough nutrients to last 4–6 weeks, after which your crops may need more nutrients and could fail to thrive unless you take steps to support them.
• Mix slow-release fertilizer pellets into the soil mix at the time of planting, which will feed your plants all season.
• Apply a liquid fertilizer weekly to give a boost to hungry crops, such as tomatoes and zucchini.
• Spread mulch or slow-release fertilizer on the soil of plants that have been growing in pots for more than one year.

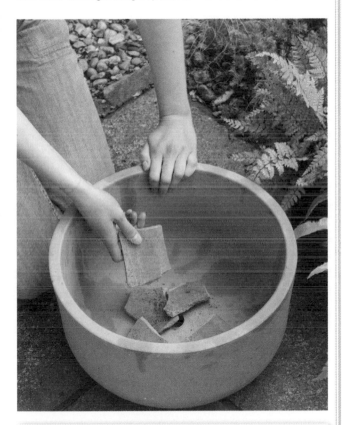

GOOD DRAINAGE

Plants need good drainage to keep their roots from becoming waterlogged, so ensure any container you use has ample holes in the bottom. If it does not, carefully make some, using a drill. To stop the drainage holes from becoming blocked with soil mix, cover them with pieces of a broken pot or bits of broken-up styrofoam. Some plants need very good drainage, so mix coarse grit into their potting mix.

Preparing to plant

KEEPING ROOTS COOL Metal containers are poorly insulated, allowing the soil mix inside to become warm, which plants don't like. Prevent this by lining the insides with bubble wrap before filling with soil mix, taking care not to block the drainage holes. Pierce some holes to ensure proper drainage is possible.

REUSING OLD POTTING MIX If you've used multipurpose potting mix to grow quick-growing crops, such as microgreens, that have only been in it for a few weeks, you could reuse it. Pick out any plant debris, add slow-release fertilizer, and top it up with soil mix. Any soil mix used for longer than a few weeks is best discarded.

POSITIONING LARGE CONTAINERS is easiest to do before you fill them with potting mix.

What should I grow?

....what you like eating!

Good to eat

If **time** and **space** are limited, grow the **fruit** and **vegetables** that you find the **most delicious**, whether that's **tasty peas** or **juicy** apples. As long as you can **provide** the **right conditions**, simply grow the **crops** you **love** the most.

Suit your site

If your **yard** is **shady**, sun-loving crops like **peppers** aren't for you, but there are **loads** of **other things** you can grow **instead**. To **enjoy** the best **harvest**, choose crops that **suit** the **conditions** your garden provides (*see pp.224–241*).

Best fresh

Think about crops that are **best** eaten **fresh**, like **peas** and **sweet corn**, or those that are **expensive** to buy. You can even grow crops you **rarely** see **sold** in stores, such as deliciously **aromatic** herbs, like **sorrel** and **sweet cicely**.

Time wise

Choose **fast-growing** crops to help **make the most** of the space you have. **Speedy** crops, such as **pea shoots**, are **ready to pick** in a matter of **weeks**, giving you time to **grow something** else **in the same space** (*see pp.50–51*).

What plants can you fit in?

Use this **guide** to **help you** decide the best **crops** for your **growing space**. Don't **forget** to consider the **places where** you can **set** pots, **hang** baskets, and **train climbing** crops **vertically**.

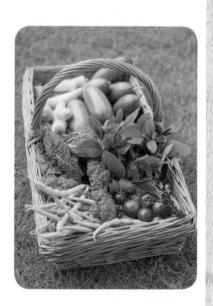

CROP	Planting distance (in/cm)	Height (in/cm)	Plant characteristics
Tomatoes—bush	18–36 (45–90)	12–48 (30–120)	Dense and bushy
Tomatoes—cordon	16–18 (40–45)	60–72 (150–180)	Upright and leafy
Sweet peppers	18–24 (45–60)	24–36 (60–90)	Dense and bushy
Chili peppers	14–18 (35–45)	12–36 (30–90)	Dense and bushy
Eggplant	24–30 (60–75)	24–36 (60–90)	Dense and bushy
Zucchini	36 (90)	12–18 (30–45)	Leafy and spreading
Summer squash	36 (90)	12–18 (30–45)	Leafy and spreading
Cucumbers	18–36 (45–90)	72 (180)	Climbing or spreading
Cucamelons	12–16 (30–40)	8ft (2.5m)	Climbing or spreading
Pea shoots	¾ (2)	2–4 (5–10)	Upright and leafy
Peas	2–5 (5–13)	24–48 (60–120)	Climbing or upright
Green beans	2–4 (5–10)	39–72 (100–180)	Dense and climbing
Runner beans	6 (15)	72 (180)	Dense and climbing
Broad beans	10 (25)	36–48 (90–120)	Upright and leafy
Radishes	½ (1)	6 (15)	Low and leafy
Carrots	2–4 (5–10)	6–12 (15–30)	Low and leafy
Beets	2–4 (5–10)	10–14 (25–35)	Low and leafy
Potatoes	12–16 (30–40)	30–36 (75–90)	Dense and bushy
Turnips	3–5 (8–13)	12–18 (30–45)	Low and leafy
Kohlrabi	10 (25)	12–18 (30–45)	Low and leafy
Florence fennel	12 (30)	24–36 (60–90)	Low and leafy
Green onions	½ (1)	10–14 (25–35)	Low and leafy
Garlic	8 (20)	12–14 (30–35)	Upright and sparse
Leeks	6–8 (15–20)	18–24 (45–60)	Upright and leafy
Lettuce	6–14 (15–35)	6–12 (15–30)	Low and leafy
Spinach	6 (15)	12–24 (30–60)	Upright and leafy
Mustard greens	15–30 (6–12)	6–8 (15–20)	Low and leafy
Arugula	15 (6)	6–8 (15–20)	Low and leafy
Swiss chard	8 (20)	18–24 (45–60)	Upright and leafy
Bok choy	4–10 (10–25)	12–26 (30–65)	Low and leafy
Endive	10 (25)	14–16 (35–40)	Low and leafy
Chicory	12 (30)	16–20 (40–50)	Low and leafy
Kale	24 (60)	20–36 (50–90)	Upright and leafy
Sprouting broccoli	24 (60)	36–48 (90–120)	Upright and leafy
Sweet corn	14–18 (35–45)	60–72 (150–180)	Upright and leafy

Small space rating (see p.224)	Small pots	Large pots	Window boxes	Hanging baskets	Raised beds
★★★		✓	Miniature	Trailing	✓
★★★		✓			✓
★★		✓	✓		✓
★★★	✓	✓	✓		✓
★		✓	✓		✓
★★		✓			✓
★★		✓			✓
★★★		✓			✓
★		✓		✓	✓
★★★	✓	✓	✓	✓	✓
★★		✓			✓
★★★		✓			✓
★★★		✓			✓
★		✓			✓
★★★	Baby	✓	Round	Round	✓
★★	Round	✓	Baby or round	Baby	✓
★★★	Baby	✓	Baby		✓
★		✓			✓
★★		Round	Baby		✓
★★★		✓			✓
★		✓			✓
★★	✓	✓	✓	✓	✓
★		✓	✓		✓
★★		✓			✓
★★★	✓	✓	✓		✓
★★		✓	✓		✓
★★★	✓	✓	✓	✓	✓
★★★	✓	✓	✓	✓	✓
★★★	✓	✓	✓		✓
★★★	✓	✓		✓	✓
★★		✓	✓		✓
★★		✓	✓		✓
★★		✓	✓		✓
★					✓
★		✓			✓

When growing baby crops, you can sow and plant them more closely together. However, keep them well watered, so they don't compete with one another for moisture.

HERBS	Planting distance (in/cm)	Height (in/cm)	Plant characteristics	Small space rating	SUITABLE FOR				
					Small pots	Large Pots	Window boxes	Hanging baskets	Raised beds
French sorrel	12 (30)	12–20 (30–50)	Upright and leafy	★★★		✓			✓
Lovage	24 (60)	72 (180)	Upright and leafy	★★★		✓			✓
Parsley	6 (15)	12–36 (30–90)	Low and leafy	★★	✓	✓	✓	✓	✓
Sweet cicely	24 (60)	39–72 (100–180)	Upright and sparse	★★★		✓			✓
Fennel	18 (45)	48–60 (120–150)	Upright and feathery	★★★		✓			✓
Starflower	8 (20)	12–39 (30–100)	Low and leafy	★★★		✓	✓		✓
Sage	16 (40)	18–36 (45–90)	Leafy shrub	★★		✓	✓		✓
Lavender	20 (50)	18–48 (45–120)	Dense shrub	★★		✓	✓		✓
Rosemary	16 (40)	24–48 (60–120)	Upright shrub	★★		✓	✓		✓
Basil	10 (25)	12–24 (30–60)	Low and leafy	★★★	✓	✓	✓	✓	✓
African basil	12 (30)	20–24 (50–60)	Low and leafy	★★		✓	✓		✓
Mint	12 (30)	24–48 (60–120)	Upright and leafy	★★★		✓	✓		✓
French tarragon	24 (60)	24–36 (60–90)	Upright and leafy	★★★		✓	✓		✓
Chives	6 (15)	12–18 (30–45)	Upright and sparse	★★★	✓	✓	✓	✓	✓
Dill	8 (20)	24–36 (60–90)	Upright and sparse	★★★		✓	✓		✓
Marjoram	10 (25)	6–18 (15–45)	Low and leafy	★★★	✓	✓	✓	✓	✓
Thyme	12 (30)	2–10 (5–25)	Creeping	★★★	✓	✓	✓	✓	✓
Coriander	12 (30)	12–24 (30–60)	Low and leafy	★★★	✓	✓	✓	✓	✓

FRUIT	Planting distance (in/cm)	Height (in/cm)	Plant characteristics	Small space rating	Small pots	Large Pots	Window boxes	Hanging baskets	Raised beds
Strawberries (inc. alpine types)	12–16 (30–40)	6–12 (15–30)	Low and leafy	★★	✓	✓	✓	✓	✓
Raspberries	14–18 (35–45)	48–60 (120–150)	Dense and upright	★★★		✓			✓
Japanese wineberries	8–11ft (2.5–3.5m)	6–10ft (1.8–3m)	Unruly shrub, can be trained along poles and wires	★★		✓			✓
Blackberries	8–11ft (2.5–3.5m)	6–10ft (1.8–3m)	Unruly shrub, can be trained along poles and wires	★★		✓			✓
Blueberries	5ft (1.5m)	36–60 (90–150)	Bushy	★		✓			✓
Apples—on dwarf rootstocks	6–12ft (1.8–3.6m)	6–10ft (2–3m)	Tree	★		✓			✓
Pear—on dwarf rootstocks	6–12ft (1.8–3.6m)	6–10ft (2–3m)	Tree	★		✓			✓
Apples—trained types	8–11ft (2.5–3.5m)	Depends on type grown	Space-saving types	★★					✓

Make use of vertical surfaces to train climbing crops

Pick your crops regularly to promote a larger harvest

Plant closely and resow or plant areas after harvesting

15 Top sun-loving crops

Some plants will need at least six hours of direct sunlight per day to produce crops that develop fully and will ripen well. If your courtyard, balcony, or roof terrace is a sun trap, these plants will thrive, giving you the sweetest tasting fruit and vegetables.

1 TOMATOES There are many exciting varieties. Try 'Green Zebra' and 'Banana Legs', which you won't find in stores.

2 ZUCCHINI Sow yellow and green varieties in repeated batches for masses of this versatile crop.

3 EGGPLANT Best suited for warm climates or raising under cover, there are purple and white-fruited varieties.

4 CHILI PEPPERS Decorative and edible, the fruit develop in a stunning array of shapes, colors, and tastes.

5 SWEET PEPPERS Best in a warm spot, the brightly colored fruit will enliven any vegetable patch.

6 STRAWBERRIES The taste of summer; grow early and late varieties to extend your harvest.

7 FENNEL The feathery leaves are almost reason enough to grow this delicious anise-flavored herb.

8 BASIL As well as sweet basil, also try purple, Thai, African, and cinnamon varieties for more interesting flavors.

Others to try
- Cucumbers
- Summer squash
- Green and runner beans
- Florence fennel
- Rosemary
- Raspberries
- Garlic

15 Top shade-tolerant crops

Not all plants need full sun to grow well, and some, especially leafy crops, relish a cooler, shadier location. If your growing space is north-facing, or there are surrounding trees or buildings that block out the sun for part of the day, these crops are ideal choices.

1 LETTUCE Sow little and often for an endless supply, and plant a mix of varieties for a decorative effect.

2 SWISS CHARD The variety 'Bright Lights' has vividly colored stems that glow in the sun. It will crop into winter.

3 MUSTARD LEAVES With varied colors and textures, these spicy leaves are ideal for salads and stir-fries.

4 SPINACH Pick the leaves small and tender to use raw in salads, or let them grow larger to enjoy them cooked.

5 FALL RASPBERRIES 'Polka' produces copious amounts of huge juicy berries from late summer until fall.

6 ALPINE STRAWBERRIES These berries are small but extremely tasty. Plant them along paths or in containers.

7 RUNNER BEANS This climbing crop bears attractive red or white flowers, and an abundance of summer beans.

8 SORREL An underused, easy-to-grow perennial herb with a delicious lemony bite. Use it in salads and soups.

Others to try
- Arugula
- Parsley
- Peas
- Radishes
- Sweet cicely
- Mint
- Coriander

15 Top high-yielding crops

If you only have a limited amount of room to grow fruit and vegetables, it's important to choose those crops that make best use of the space they occupy by rewarding you with an abundant harvest. Those that crop over a long period are especially worthwhile.

1 GREEN AND RUNNER BEANS These climbing beans bear purple, yellow, or green pods for many weeks.

2 ARUGULA A dual-purpose crop, the peppery leaves are perfect for salads, while the flowers are sweet and spicy.

3 BEETS Producing two crops in one, these are grown for their leaves and roots. 'Chioggia' has striped flesh.

4 LETTUCE Delicious and decorative, only pick outer leaves for eating, or enjoy a cut-and-come-again harvest.

5 RADISHES These are swift growers—sow seed every few weeks for a ready supply of crunchy, hot bites.

6 MUSTARD LEAVES This hot and spicy leaf crop can be picked over a long period, or be resown regularly.

7 ZUCCHINI This fleshy fruit comes thick and fast in summer, more so when they are picked regularly.

8 SWISS CHARD The young fresh leaves are good for salads, while older, larger ones can be cooked like spinach.

Others to try
- Early potatoes
- Zucchini
- Spinach
- Carrots
- Microgreens
- Everlasting strawberries
- Chinese broccoli

15 Top quick-growing crops

Just as space is limited in the garden, so too is time, and it's important to take full advantage of the growing season. These are some of the quickest vegetables to grow, swiftly providing pickings from your plot, then making way, ready for you to sow more vegetables.

1 PEA SHOOTS Ready to pick in just 3 weeks, the crisp shoots are fresh and succulent. Perfect for many salads.

2 MICROGREENS Taking 3–5 weeks, these intensely flavorful mini leaves can be grown from spare seeds.

3 RADISHES Taking 4–6 weeks, sow these spicy roots in regular batches for a constant supply throughout summer.

4 ARUGULA Mature leaves are ready to eat in 4–5 weeks, and you can also use the thinnings as microgreens.

5 BOK CHOY Within 6–8 weeks, these fresh and succulent Asian greens can be eaten raw or used in stir-fries.

6 ZUCCHINI These start bearing fruit within 8–10 weeks. The male flowers can also be picked and eaten.

7 CARROTS Ready to harvest within 8–10 weeks, try mini round 'Paris Market' or multicolored 'Harlequin'.

8 CHINESE BROCCOLI Pick after 8–10 weeks, and let the stem resprout. It tastes more bitter than broccoli.

Others to try
- Swiss chard
- Beets
- Kohlrabi
- Lettuce
- Green and runner beans
- Florence fennel
- Early potatoes

15 Top easy-care crops

Some vegetables are prima donnas, demanding attention throughout their growing season. Others, however, once planted, grow very happily on their own, just waiting for you to harvest when the crop ripens. If growing them in pots, don't forget to water though!

1 RUNNER BEANS Simply plant these robust climbers at the base of a pole and look forward to a good harvest.

2 STRAWBERRIES Feed in spring, cut off any runners, and these plants will crop for several weeks.

3 FALL RASPBERRIES Once planted, mulch in spring, enjoy the fruit, then remove all stems in late winter.

4 ZUCCHINI Always water well, and feed if fruiting starts to flag. Pick zucchini small to encourage fruiting.

5 KOHLRABI Sow seeds in batches in spring and summer, then watch the unusual-looking crop develop.

6 PEA SHOOTS Soak dried peas overnight, sow, and 3 weeks later pick the shoots, once large enough to use.

7 SPROUTING BROCCOLI Slow but easy to grow, sow in spring, plant out in summer, then crop next spring.

8 SWISS CHARD This hardy crop will grow through winter, when you can harvest the leaves as you need them.

Others to try

- Beets
- Lettuce
- Carrots
- Mustard leaves
- Mint
- Sorrel
- Sweet cicely

15 Top shallow-rooted crops

Shallow-rooted vegetables are a godsend for growing on balconies, windowsills, and rooftops, where the quantity of soil, and especially its weight, is a serious consideration. All of these crops can be grown in a mere 6in (15cm) of soil, when kept well watered.

1 LETTUCE Harvest the plants as a cut-and-come-again crop, or as mature heads. Sow seed in regular batches.

2 RADISHES Small round varieties, such as 'Cherry Belle', are perfect for growing in pots and shallow beds.

3 FLORENCE FENNEL Decorative and tasty, plant them 12in (30cm) apart to allow decent-sized bulbs to develop.

4 CHIVES Both the stems and flowers of this useful perennial herb are edible. Divide congested plants in spring.

5 MUSTARD LEAVES Try growing 'Green in Snow', 'Red Giant', and 'Osaka Purple' for a mix of tastes.

6 GREEN AND RUNNER BEANS Water well and harvest regularly to grow beans well on shallower soils.

7 ALPINE STRAWBERRIES Ideal to plant along the edges of beds, these small berries are very sweet and tasty.

8 TOMATOES At home in shallow beds and grow bags, keep plants well watered and fed during the summer.

Others to try
- Peas
- Garlic
- Swiss chard
- Marigolds
- Nasturtiums
- Mint
- Sage

Making the most of your growing space

Once you have identified your growing space, the next step is to use it as productively as possible. This means squeezing in as many crops as you can, encouraging them to produce the biggest harvest possible, and ensuring the space is fully planted all season.

The **best place** to grow crops is in a **bed**, ideally a **raised** one that can be **filled** with **fertile soil** and **tended** from the **sides**, with **crops grown close together**. Dividing it into **equal** areas helps you **allocate** space to **crops** with **little waste**.

Container growing

EVEN SMALL YARDS produce bountiful crops, because fruit and vegetables can be grown just as intensively in containers as when planted in beds. Even if you don't have a single large area to devote to your crops, the growing space offered by several containers can add up significantly, as shown here. The nine containers shown on the left (*see also pp.133–155*) provide exactly the same growing space as the bed above. However, they have the advantage that you can position them around your yard, using every spot available.

Raising crops in pots to plant out when existing ones are harvested means your garden is always productive. Plan your sowing and planting in advance (see pp.224–241).

Harvesting crops all season

CROPS GROW AND MATURE at different rates, which helps you use your space and the growing season efficiently. Quick-growing crops provide several harvests in a single season, and can be planted to make use of the space around those that grow slower (*see pp.50–51*). Low-growers, such as lettuce, can be planted beneath taller crops, such as sweet corn. Don't ever waste an inch!

Extend the growing season

Seeds and plants grow quicker in warmer conditions, and there are simple ways to provide them. This will give the plants an earlier start, prolong the season, and increase your harvest.

- **Warming** the soil enables you to **sow** seeds **outside** earlier.
- Sow seeds **under cover** to give plants a **head start** in spring.
- **Cloches** and covers encourage **growth** and **allow plants** to **crop for longer**.

The seed of most crops can be sown in pots on a bright windowsill. This is ideal for those that need a long season, such as peppers.

Beating the chill

In most cases, extending the season is about eating into fall and winter by trapping warmth and protecting your plants from cold. Even tender crops can last into fall with a little help.

Covering your soil for a few weeks in late winter with sheets of black plastic warms the soil, allowing you to sow seeds directly outside sooner. This is ideal for raised beds.

Protecting plants from frost in spring and fall means they develop sooner and continue cropping longer. Crops in pots can also be brought indoors to keep them going.

Cold frames are easy to make yourself and ideal for raising plants. They offer frost protection, so can be used to grow crops, such as Swiss chard, through the winter.

Covering plants with cloches in spring guards against frost and encourages growth. Cloches can also be used to protect winter crops, such as endive and chicory.

Mini-greenhouses provide the perfect growing conditions for warmth-loving plants, like tomatoes, peppers, and eggplant. Here, they will crop sooner, better, and for longer.

Harvesting crops regularly lengthens the season by encouraging plants to replace the leaves and fruit they have lost. Of course, this doesn't apply to root crops!

Preparing your soil

Good soil is essential for producing a healthy harvest, and time spent preparing it before planting will be well rewarded. New beds can be filled with the best mix possible (*see p.23*). With existing beds, however, you need to make the most of what's already there.

Before preparing your soil, make sure you know what type you have (see p.18). Adding organic matter, such as compost, will improve drainage in heavy clay soils and make sandy soils better at retaining nutrients and moisture.

Giving your soil a makeover

When growing crops in a raised bed, you can employ the no dig approach (*see p.23*). Using this technique, well-rotted organic matter, such as garden compost or manure, is applied to the surface and left for the worms to incorporate naturally into the soil. The advantage is that the soil structure isn't damaged by digging, and the mulch can be applied around any existing crops. However, the worms don't do all the work for you, and there are further steps to improving your soil.

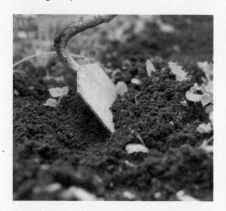

1 Start by weeding the soil thoroughly, being sure to remove any perennial weeds completely (*see pp.246–247*). Weed roots should not be composted.

2 Water the soil well, then, starting at one end of the bed, cover the surface with a deep mulch of organic matter, 4in (10cm) thick. Don't dig it in.

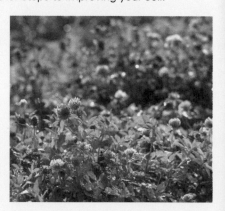

3 If the bed is going to remain empty in fall and winter, sow a green manure, such as red clover (*above*), which can be dug into the soil in spring.

Busy soil is best

Soil is a living material, and the more crops you grow, the better it becomes over time. Plant roots help to break up soil, improving its drainage and aeration, and attract beneficial soil organisms, such as fungi and bacteria. Help your soil by growing many crops.

Sowing seeds

Growing your own vegetables from seed is especially satisfying, as it allows you to nurture your plants from the very beginning. It is easy to do in most cases, and has many practical advantages. Perennial crops and soft fruit are best grown from plants, however.

Sowing **crops from seed** allows **you** to **grow** the **widest range possible**, including **unusual varieties** you **won't see** in **stores**. It also **enables** you to grow a **number of plants** very **cheaply**. Many crops can **only be** grown from **seed**.

Seeds in outdoor pots

Seeds can be sown directly into pots outside in a similar way as in a bed. Fill the container with soil mix and water it well. Once it has drained, either make furrows in the soil mix surface, or sow seeds onto the surface and cover them with more potting mix. Water the seeds, then wait.

Sowing outdoors

The easiest way to sow seeds is directly where they are to grow outside. Hardy seeds can be sown while the weather is still chilly if covered with fabric. For tender crops, wait until the last frost has passed.

1 When sowing into a raised bed, prepare the soil first by removing any weeds and rocks. Rake the surface level, and break up any clumps to create a fine consistency.

2 Using string, mark out where the seeds will be sown. Then, make furrows (shallow grooves) with a dibble or trowel to the depth given on the seed packet.

3 Small seeds should be thinly sown along the furrow—larger ones can be placed individually. Refer to the seed packet for the correct planting distances.

4 Cover the seeds over with soil and water them in gently using a can with a fine nozzle. Once the seedlings emerge, thin them out to the recommended spacings.

Sowing under cover

Sowing seeds indoors gives you an early start but you will need somewhere to grow the seedlings on under cover.

1 Fill small pots or flats with multipurpose soil mix. Water well and leave it to drain. Sow seeds lightly onto the soil mix and cover with more potting mix to the depth given on the seed packet.

2 Cover the seeds with a clear plastic bag to help retain moisture and place them somewhere warm and light. Check daily, and when seedlings appear, remove the plastic bag. Keep them moist as the seedlings grow.

3 Once the seedlings have two pairs of leaves, transplant them into flats, spacing them out with room to grow, or into individual pots. Alternatively, thin the seedlings out in their first flat.

4 Grow the seedlings under cover. When they are large enough, or the risk of frost has passed, acclimatize them to life outside. Put them outside by day, inside at night, for ten days.

Sowing seeds in succession

Most seeds are sown from spring to late summer.
Sow all types of crops successionally, in small frequent
batches, for constant harvests in summer and fall.

1 Quick- growing crops that mature a few weeks after sowing are ideal for successional sowing, and include pea shoots, microgreens, and radishes (*left*). These can be sown directly into your bed or in containers. Sow the seeds as shown on the packet instructions.

2 The aim is to promote rapid growth so the plants can soon be harvested. To do this, thin the seedlings so those remaining have space to grow and don't have to compete for moisture and nutrients. Keep them well watered and fed, and watch out for pests.

3 Harvest the crops as soon as they reach a usable size, freeing up space in your bed or container. Refresh the soil by removing any plant debris, and lightly turn it. You can sow a new batch of radish seeds, repeating this process as long as the season lasts.

Crop rotation

In a traditional vegetable garden, you should not grow the same crops in the same area year after year. Doing so depletes the soil of the nutrients that crop requires, and also risks attracting specific pests and diseases that attack it.

Most raised beds are too small to support effective crop rotation, since the plants grow so closely together. Instead, clear plant debris to prevent diseases, control pests, and feed the soil each year.

If crops in your raised bed are attacked by soilborne diseases, such as clubroot (see p.244), consider replacing the soil completely.

Growing crops between crops

Otherwise known as intercropping, this approach allows you to make use of the temporary spaces around and between crops that are tall and airy or slow growing.

Taller crops, such as **sweet corn**, leave **useful space** at their **base**, which you can **use** for **low-growers**, such as **beets**. **Likewise**, use any **gaps** around **slow** crops, like **sprouting broccoli**, to grow **speedier** vegetables, such as **radishes**.

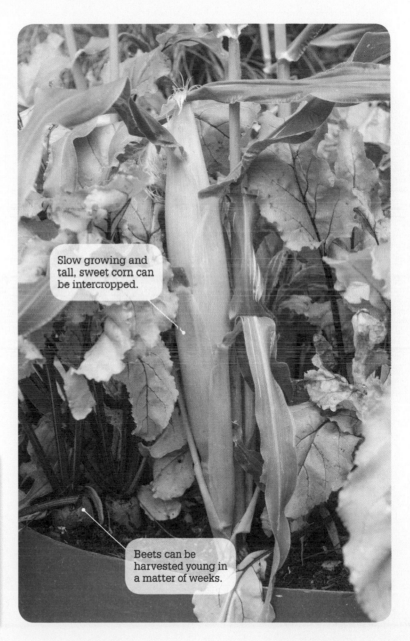

Slow growing and tall, sweet corn can be intercropped.

Beets can be harvested young in a matter of weeks.

Crop guide

- Tall crops: Sweet corn, kale, and sprouting broccoli
- Low-growing crops: Radishes, zucchini, squash, and carrots
- Slow-growing crops: Kale, sprouting broccoli, sweet corn, and peppers
- Speedy crops: Pea shoots, radishes, baby carrots, microgreens, and arugula

Feeding and watering

To reap the largest harvest possible from containers and raised beds, it is essential to water and feed your crops well. Keep them nourished and they will nourish you in return.

Fertilizing your crops

All fruit and vegetables require regular feeding as they develop, but it is important to use the correct type of fertilizer for the crops you are growing.

1 Liquid feed provides an instant boost to your crops. It is short-lived, however, so you need to apply it regularly—usually weekly.

2 Mulching with compost is ideal for slow-growing and perennial crops, because it provides nutrients slowly and over a long period.

3 Leaf crops, such as Swiss chard and lettuce, require plenty of nitrogen to grow well. Feed them using a balanced liquid fertilizer.

4 Fruiting crops, like zucchini, need potassium to flower and fruit well. Feed them using liquid tomato feed, which has potassium.

Effective watering

Even though they may get rained on, your crops rely on you for water, especially those in containers.

1 Water seedlings using a watering can with a fine nozzle to prevent damaging or washing them away.

2 Direct the water at the base of older plants so it soaks down to the roots. Avoid wetting the leaves.

3 Insert funnels made from cut-off plastic bottles to help water thirsty crops more thoroughly.

4 Conserve moisture in the soil by mulching the surface around plants. This reduces evaporation.

Micro irrigation kits

If you have a lot of containers, consider installing a simple micro irrigation system connected to a timer. You can lay seep hoses on raised beds, connected to a timer, that will water your crops automatically.

Beneficial insects

All fruiting crops, such as zucchini and strawberries, need insects to pollinate their flowers before they can produce their fruit. Attracting pollinators into your garden by planting nectar-rich flowers will help to increase your harvest. Some pollinators are also predatory, and will help to control pests, including aphids.

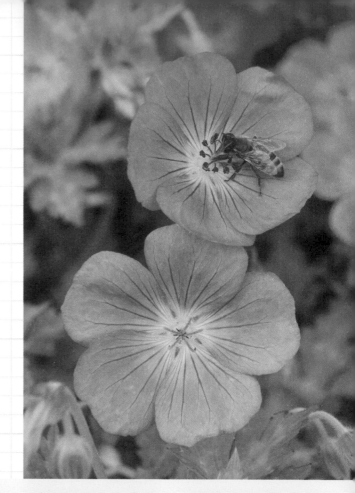

Plants for pollinators

• Pollinating insects prefer simple, single flowers that they can easily access. Avoid those with complex double blooms.

• To attract insects throughout the growing season, plant a variety of flowers that lasts from spring to fall.

• Include spring-flowering bulbs and blossom-rich trees, summer herbs, and fall perennials.

Lavender

California poppies

Fennel

Hollyhocks

Love-in-a-mist

Apple blossoms

Making use of garden leftovers

- When harvesting your crops, don't be in a hurry to tidy up right away. The flowers of many herbs and vegetables are loved by pollinating insects.
- Carrots and parsnips are biennial, but are normally pulled before they flower. However, bees love their blooms, so leave some in to flower next year.
- Mustard leaf bears yellow flowers if not cropped, which attract pollinators and are edible.

Cornflowers

Borage

Crocus

Giant hyssop

Insect allies

By creating areas for insects, such as ladybugs and lacewings, to overwinter, they will be on hand in spring to control your pests and pollinate your crops.

Bees
Wild bees hibernate in holes in the ground and in trees, although you can also help by providing a "bee hotel." Feeding on nectar and pollen during summer, they are vital crop pollinators.

Hoverflies
Resembling wasps, these are doubly beneficial in the garden. Adults pollinate flowers and the larvae avidly feed on aphids.

Butterflies and moths
These pollinate flowers and are a welcome sight in the garden. They also attract beneficial birds that feed on the caterpillars.

Watch and learn

Whether you're at a nursery or visiting a garden, take note of the plants that pollinators feed on. They will guide you to the best plants to grow. Buddleia bushes are always swathed in butterflies, and borage seems to be bee heaven.

Companion planting

Controlling damaging pests is essential to growing the biggest harvest, and there are certain plants that do some of the work for you.

While **pests flock** to **certain** plants, they **steer clear** of **others**. Grow **pest magnets away** from your crops as **a cunning lure**, and **use** those they **hate** as a **barrier**. You can also **grow plants** to attract **pest predators**.

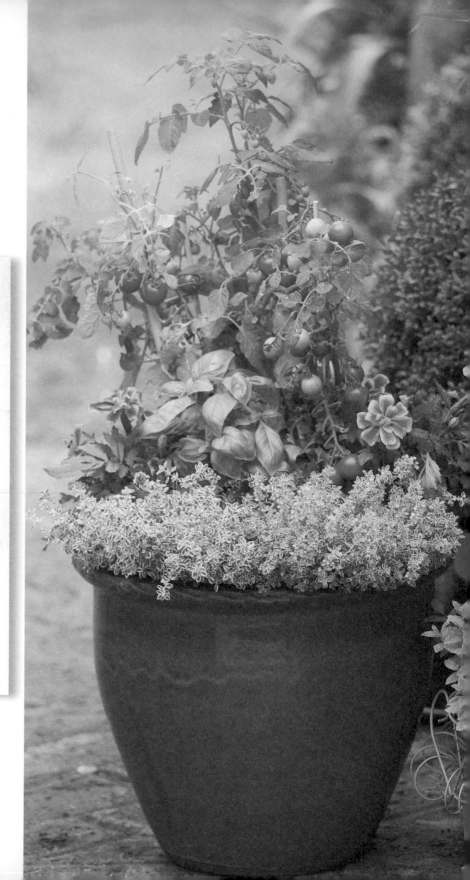

Your growing allies

Grow these plants in your beds and containers to protect your crops from pests. All except poached egg plant are also edible, doubling their value.

MARIGOLDS These edible flowers attract aphid-eating hoverflies.

CHIVES Their onion scent helps prevent carrot rust flies from finding your crop.

POACHED EGG PLANT This annual attracts hoverflies that avidly feed on aphids. Sow it directly at the edge of your beds or grow it in containers placed near your crops.

GARLIC Grow carrots next to garlic to mask their scent from pesky carrot rust flies.

NASTURTIUMS Grow these to lure aphids away from your vulnerable crops.

THYME Plant this scented herb near your crops to help fend off aphid attacks.

FRENCH MARIGOLDS Use these pungent plants to help ward off whiteflies.

BASIL Plant this herb alongside tomatoes to help repel aphid attack.

MINT Plant pots of scented mint near your beds and containers to deter aphids.

SMALL SPACE PROJECTS

Balcony planter

Hanging a planter on railings makes great use of space on a balcony. Fill it with vining crops, like trailing tomatoes.

Materials

Planter
Bubble wrap
Multipurpose
potting mix
Liquid tomato feed

Plants

Trailing tomatoes
Dianthus

Find a sturdy planter with strong hooks and hang it facing onto your balcony so you can enjoy the display, care for your plants, and harvest the fruit easily.

1 If you're using a metal container, line it with a piece of bubble wrap to prevent the roots from heating up in hot sun. Make holes in the wrap so the planter drains freely.

2 Fill the container with multipurpose soil mix, finishing 2in (5cm) below the rim to allow space for easier watering.

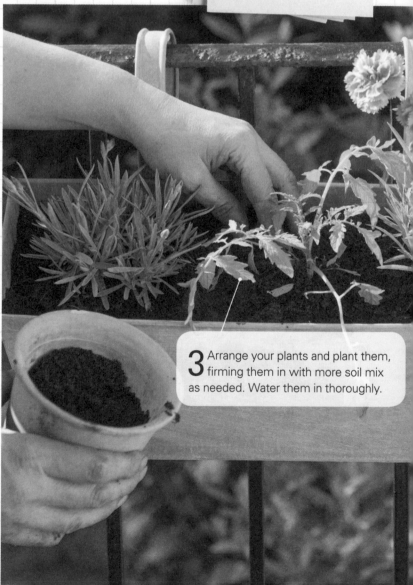

3 Arrange your plants and plant them, firming them in with more soil mix as needed. Water them in thoroughly.

4 Keep the plants well watered, even in rainy spells. Begin feeding the tomato plant with liquid tomato feed weekly as soon as the first flowers begin to appear.

Care Advice
Deadheading Pick off dead flower heads to keep dianthus blooming throughout the summer.

Ripening At the end of the season, add green tomatoes to a fruit bowl with apples and bananas to help them ripen, or make chutney.

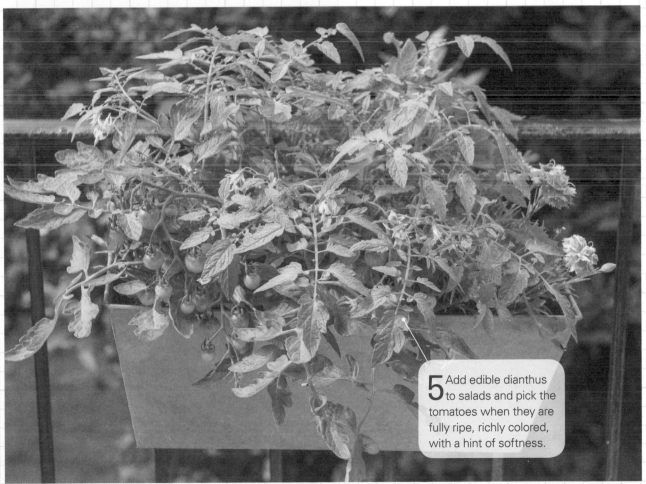

5 Add edible dianthus to salads and pick the tomatoes when they are fully ripe, richly colored, with a hint of softness.

Strawberry colander

Store-bought strawberries never taste as good as those you pick yourself, and here is a way to grow them with style in a small space—by using a retro colander as a hanging basket.

Materials

Vintage or retro-style metal colander
Hanging basket bracket
Hanging basket chains
Multipurpose soil mix
Bubble wrap
Scissors
Watering can

Plants

5 x strawberry plants

Combine summer-fruiting and perennial strawberry varieties (see p.233) for the longest crop, lasting from midsummer to fall. Pick the berries when they are firm and bright red.

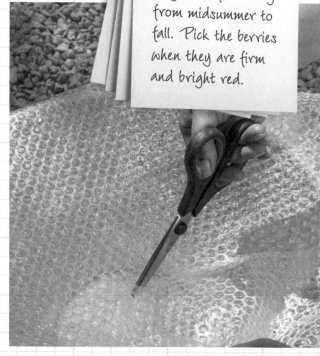

2 Measure out the bubble wrap to fit the container and don't forget to put holes in it to let water drain through. Waterlogged plants will quickly begin to die off.

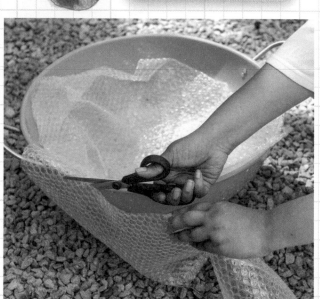

1 Look for a good-sized metal colander with plenty of room in it. The drainage holes make it ideal as a planter but it will need insulating to protect the roots from overheating.

3 Smooth out the bumps and ridges to allow maximum room for potting mix. This is a restricted space and you need to make use of every bit of it when you fill it.

4 Fill the colander halfway with soil mix and position the strawberries evenly on the base so that they will sit about 1¼in (3 cm) below the top of the container.

5 Remove the pots. If you find the roots have become pot-bound, tease them out with your fingers before planting to help them grow out naturally into the fresh soil mix.

6 Fill in the gaps around the plants with soil mix and firm it in well, finishing the layer about 1in (2.5cm) below the rim of the colander to allow space for watering.

7 Give the plants a really good soak, and leave the colander on the ground until all the water has been absorbed. Add more soil mix if it has settled and left gaps between plants.

Others to try

Aromatic trailing and bushy herbs, such as oregano and basil, would be ideal to grow instead of strawberries.

Trailing tomatoes make good hanging displays, but use just one plant per colander and water without fail every day.

Care Advice

Lifespan Strawberries are perennials and will bear some fruit in their first year, but crop better in the second and third.

Runners After fruiting, plants put out runners to make new plants. Snip them off to conserve the plants' energy.

8 Space the hanging basket chains evenly and attach them by clipping them to the holes in the colander. If using summer-fruiting strawberries, hang them in full sun.

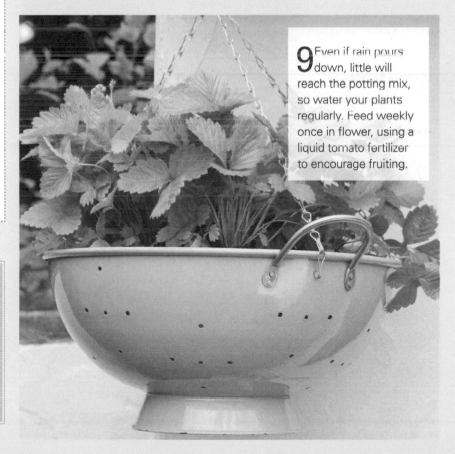

9 Even if rain pours down, little will reach the potting mix, so water your plants regularly. Feed weekly once in flower, using a liquid tomato fertilizer to encourage fruiting.

Balcony saddlebags

Hanging a fabric saddlebag over a railing will double your growing space with crops on both sides of the rail.

Materials

Sturdy fabric, roughly 3 x4ft (1x1.2m) per saddlebag	Hammer
	Scissors
	Chalk pencil
Tape measure	Hanging basket liner
Heavy-duty rivet kit	Water-absorbing beads
Ruler	Multipurpose soil mix

Plants

Tomato 'Bitonto'	Swiss chard
Trailing tomatoes	Sorrel
Strawberries	Arugula
Basil (green and purple)	Red giant mustard leaf
Oregano	Marigolds
Mint	Cornflowers

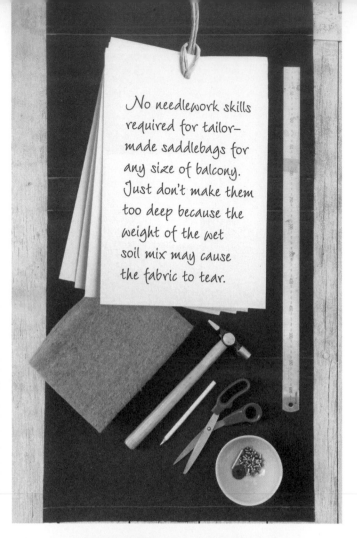

No needlework skills required for tailor-made saddlebags for any size of balcony. Just don't make them too deep because the weight of the wet soil mix may cause the fabric to tear.

1 Cut out the cloth to size and hem the short sides by folding in ¾in (2cm) of fabric three times and hammering in rivets, 4in (10cm) apart.

2 Leave 2½in (6cm) clear at each end. Draw two lines in the center of the cloth to accommodate the width of your railing and allow the bags to hang, then bring the riveted ends up to the lines.

3 Turn the cloth to work on the long sides. Fold over 1¼in (3cm) of fabric twice along each of the long sides to make seams and create the bags. Rivet them in place.

4 Cut a length of hanging-basket liner and fold it inside each bag to retain moisture. It should set just below the lip of the bag.

5 For an extra boost in moisture retention, mix ¼oz (5g) of water-absorbing beads into 1 gallon (5 liters) of multipurpose soil mix before you use it to fill the bags.

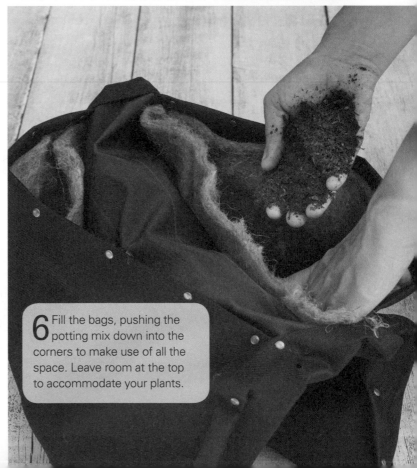

6 Fill the bags, pushing the potting mix down into the corners to make use of all the space. Leave room at the top to accommodate your plants.

7 Hang the bags on the rail. Plant sun-loving crops and flowers on the outside and shade-tolerant plants facing inward.

8 Firm in the plants with more soil mix and water them well. Keep watering throughout the season, even if it rains.

Planting combinations

Think of your saddlebags as miniature English gardens—a traditional mix of vegetables, fruit, and flowers that complement each other perfectly.

Marigolds and verbena add a splash of color to this saddlebag, planted with zesty French sorrel.

Salad bag on the inside has mustard greens and Swiss chard with a trailing tomato out front.

Mediterranean bag features a dwarf bush tomato, purple and green basil, and oregano.

Strawberries do best on the sunny side with a cluster of marigolds. Cornflowers and mint form a backdrop.

Care Advice

Topping off Keep the bags topped off with soil mix if any gets washed away to keep the weight of each pocket even.

Tidy up Remove damaged or dying foliage and deadhead flowering plants to encourage them to bloom repeatedly.

Corn oil drum

Sun-loving sweet corn needs a hot summer to do well. It grows tall so pick a deep, roomy container—an oil drum is perfect—and place it in a warm, sunny spot.

Sweet corn is slow growing and casts little shade, which makes it a great candidate for intercropping. Try beets, lettuce, arugula, parsley, or mustard greens.

Tools and materials

A large container at least 16in (40cm) in diameter with drainage holes in the bottom
Multipurpose soil mix

Liquid fertilizer
Watering can

Plants and seeds

Small sweet corn plants (purchased or grown indoors from seed)
Beet seeds

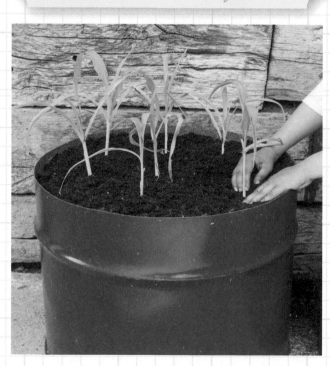

1 **You can** grow sweet corn from seed indoors from mid-spring onward, or buy young plants. Plant out in a sheltered spot in full sun when danger of frost has passed.

2 Space the plants evenly in a block rather than in a row. This will help wind pollination between the male and female flowers, which is essential for kernels to form.

Care Advice

Planting Sweet corn dislikes moving so don't let young plants become too big before you plant them outdoors.

Harvesting Most plants produce one or two cobs in August or September. Pull apart the leaves to check for pale yellow kernels, then twist the ripe cob off at its base.

3 Water the plants in well and continue to keep the drum well watered and free of weeds. Remove any weak or failing plants to create more space, if need be.

4 Thinly scatter beet seeds (or seeds for fast-growing salads or herbs) between the corn. When seedlings appear, thin them out to their correct planting distances.

5 After 4–6 weeks, the sturdy plants will be depleting the nutrients in the potting mix. Feed them once a week with a liquid fertilizer to boost crop production.

6 Pick some of the earthy young beet leaves for salads. When the beets are ready to harvest a few weeks later, pull them out gently to avoid disturbing the corn.

Carrot oil drum

Sow seeds thinly in multipurpose soil mix in rows or circles. Planting your crop high up may help to protect it from carrot rust flies, which fly close to the ground.

Lightly cover the seeds with soil mix, and water them in thoroughly using a watering can with a fine nozzle. Keep the growing plants well watered.

Thin out baby carrots regularly to eat raw in salads and make room for the full-sized carrots to develop. You can eat the carrot tops too—they taste a bit like parsley.

7 For the sweetest cobs, pick them as soon as their silky tassels start to turn brown and eat them within 24 hours. If cobs are left too long, their sugar turns to starch.

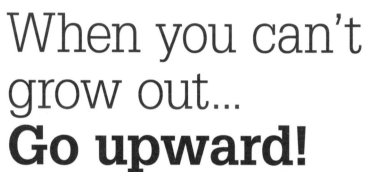

When you can't grow out...
Go upward!

Your **ground space** may be **limited**, but by growing **crops vertically**, you can **double**, or even **triple**, the **area** you have. Instead of placing a **raised bed** at the base of this fence (*right*), **lean-to shelves** provide **far more** space. Growing **climbing crops** up supports also maximizes **space efficiency**. Requiring the same amount of soil as a **few lettuce plants**, you can enjoy crops like **runner beans** to **harvest all summer long**.

Cucumber trellis

This unusual cucumber needs little space to produce garlands of globes that taste as good as they look. For a bumper crop, choose a warm, sheltered spot.

Materials

A large container, at least
12in (30cm) in diameter
Multipurpose soil mix
Slow-release fertilizer
3 x bamboo poles
Garden twine

Watering can
Liquid tomato fertilizer
Bubble wrap

Plants

Cucumber 'Crystal Apple'
(Grown from seed or bought as a small plant)

'Crystal Apple' may look unusual but it has a similar taste and texture to other cucumbers. Its advantage is that it grows well outdoors. You could also use ridge varieties.

1 Fill a large container with multipurpose soil mix and mix in some slow-release fertilizer to feed the plant. If you are using a metal container, line it with bubble wrap (*see p.29*).

2 Push the bamboo poles into the soil mix and tie them together at the top to form a tepee. Wind string around it from bottom to top for the cucumber to climb up.

3 Either grow your own cucumber plant from seed, sown individually in pots indoors mid-spring, or buy a plant. Harden it off and plant it outside after the last frost.

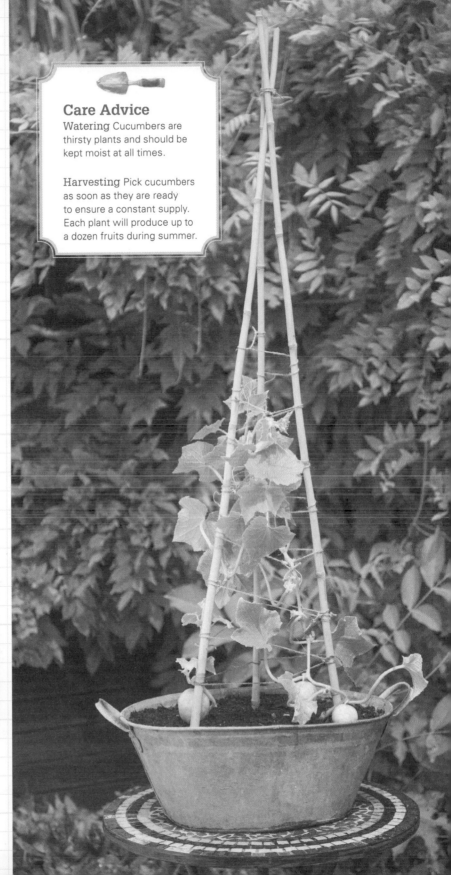

Care Advice

Watering Cucumbers are thirsty plants and should be kept moist at all times.

Harvesting Pick cucumbers as soon as they are ready to ensure a constant supply. Each plant will produce up to a dozen fruits during summer.

4 Firm the plant into the soil mix and water it in well. Guide the growing tips onto the string to help the plant put out tendrils and climb the tepee.

5 Water regularly and feed weekly with tomato fertilizer once the first flowers appear. Harvest the cucumbers as soon as they are ripe and large enough to use.

Ladder shelves

These decorative shelves, filled with vibrant flowers and crops, are a perfect way to create valuable growing space on your patio.

Materials

2 x wooden ladders
3 x scaffolding boards
Approximately 20 pots

Multipurpose soil mix
Liquid plant fertilizer

Plants and seeds

Trailing tomatoes
Cucamelon
Purple basil
Marigolds
Sweet Williams
Violas

Lettuce
Strawberries
Chili peppers
Mint
Thyme
Mustard greens

Try auctions, flea markets, and yard sales for ladders and planks, and unusual containers in all sizes and colors. Paint ladders and shelves to fit your garden color scheme.

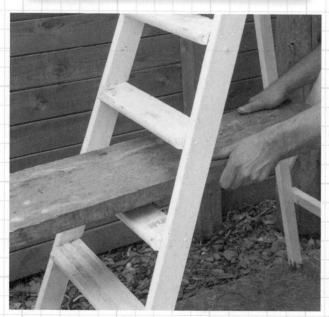

1 Place the ladders on a firm surface, facing each other, and in a sunny and sheltered spot. Evenly position the scaffolding boards to sit securely on the ladder rungs.

2 Fill a container with soil mix and use a dibble to make evenly spaced holes for larger seeds, like nasturtiums. Cover them over with potting mix and water in well.

3 To sow fine seeds, spread them over the surface of moist soil mix and cover them to the depth given on the packet. Keep them moist and thin once germinated.

4 Plant young plants or potted herbs outdoors after the last frost. Release the plant gently, surround the root ball with extra soil mix in a larger pot, and firm it in. Water well.

SOWING MICROGREENS

Microgreens are a quick and delicious crop to grow. Try all types of seeds for these tiny, intense leaves, such as basil, mustard greens, kale, and arugula. Once cropped, replace with another sowing of seeds. By repeatedly sowing every few weeks, you'll have these tasty leaves all summer long.

Caring for your plants

Continually deadhead violas, marigolds, and Sweet Williams so they continue flowering all summer.

Feed tomatoes with a liquid high-potassium fertilizer each week once the first flowers have appeared.

Pinch off the growing tips of the basil plants to encourage new sideshoots and strong, bushy growth.

5 Water the plants even when it rains since pots on lower levels may be in a rain shadow.

Easy lean-to shelves

Shelves are a great way to make use of sunny walls for growing crops in pots. Simple lean-to shelves that rest against the wall are especially simple to install.

Materials

Lean-to ladder kit
10–15 assorted pots
Multipurpose soil mix
Power drill
Screwdriver and screws
Screw anchors

Plants and seeds

Thyme, basil, and chives
Strawberries
Chili peppers
Carrot, beet, and
lettuce seeds
Plants with edible flowers

Lean-to shelving units are widely available as kits. Be sure to choose one that is sturdy enough to take the weight of your pots, and is suitable for outdoor use.

1 Choose a kit that fits neatly into the space available and make sure that it is the type that leans against the wall. Follow the instructions to assemble it.

Care Advice

Watering To ensure larger containers don't become too heavy for their shelves when wet, place them on the ground when watering them.

Feeding Feed weekly with a liquid fertilizer. Use a balanced feed for leafy crops and tomato fertilizer for fruiting plants.

2 Place the shelves against a sunny wall, making sure the base is on level ground and is stable, with both sides resting flat against the wall. Fix it securely to the wall.

3 Ensure the pots you are using have drainage holes. If they don't, carefully make some.

SHELF LIFE

Use your own judgment, but it is usually best to put heavier plants nearer the bottom and smaller, trailing plants closer to the top of the shelves.

4 Seeds of many crops, such as carrots, can be sown directly into containers. Sprinkle the seeds finely over the soil mix, cover them lightly, and water in well.

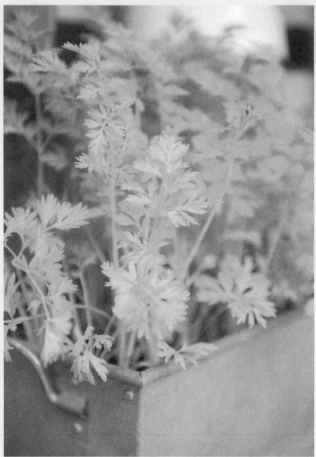

5 Keep the seeds moist until they germinate, then thin the seedlings out to leave the strongest plants. Continue to thin, leaving the rest to grow until they are harvested.

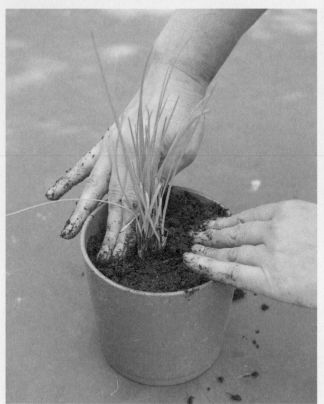

6 Repot herbs and flowers bought as young plants into containers filled with soil mix. Keep the neck of the plant at the same level as it was in its pot, and firm it in.

7 Before you place your pots on the shelves, water them well. This way water and soil will not drip onto the plants below. If you want to keep the shelves clean, continue to put your smaller pots on the ground each time you water them.

8 Turn the containers regularly to allow each side to face the sun and help the plants to grow straight. Check crops regularly to see if they are ready to be pulled or picked.

9 Fast-growing leafy crops, such as herbs and salad leaves, can soon outgrow their allotted space on the shelves, so harvest them regularly. This will keep them cropping, too.

10 Plants that appreciate the warmth and shelter provided by a wall are ideal for shelf life. Chili peppers are a great choice; they will flower and fruit continually, so pick them regularly and dry them for winter use. Other good plants for a low shelf include blueberries, sweet peppers, and dwarf bush tomatoes.

11 Siting trailing fruit, such as strawberries, high up on the ladder enhances this attractive feature. Growing strawberries above ground also keeps the fruit clean and away from pests, although check your shelves regularly for climbing slugs and snails. Mix in pinks and marigolds for a kitchen garden effect.

Bicycle wheel trellis

Pinned onto a sunny wall or fence, old bicycle wheels create a clever and creative trellis. The spokes are ideal for cucumber tendrils to cling to and climb.

Materials

3 x bicycle wheels
3 x large-headed long nails
U-shaped metal pins
Large container
Small pole
Soft string

Hammer
Multipurpose soil mix
Liquid tomato fertilizer

Plants

1 x Climbing cucumber
(Raise from seed or buy.)

Choose any ridge variety of cucumber, since these are specially selected for growing outdoors. Those with smaller fruit, such as 'Burpless Tasty Green', are prolific.

2 Hammer a long nail with a large head through the hub of each wheel. Tack extra fixing pins over some of the spokes that lie flat against the fence.

1 Find a warm, sheltered spot next to a sturdy fence or wall and experiment with different arrangements of wheels to allow height and space for the plant to climb.

Care Advice

Pinching off the growing tip of the plant as soon as it reaches the top of your trellis will encourage sideshoots and bushy growth across the wheels.

Powdery mildew is a white powdery coating that appears on leaves, often when a plant is underwatered. Remove damaged leaves as soon as you spot it.

3 Position the wheels so that they overlap a little and provide full support to your plant. Ensure they cannot turn in the wind, which could damage the plant stems.

4 Wait until all risk of frost has passed before planting out. Keep the soil mix at the same level as the neck of the plant to avoid neck rot. Firm the plant in and water it well.

5 A small bamboo pole will support the plant and help it to reach the trellis. Keep the plant watered, and protect it from pests, such as slugs, which feast on young growth.

6 As soon as the plant reaches its first wheel, tie it in loosely with soft string—then watch it grow. It will put out tendrils and climb the trellis rapidly on its own.

7 Remember to keep watering, even during wet spells. Once the first flowers appear, feed the plant weekly with a liquid tomato fertilizer to encourage a large harvest.

8 Cucumbers mature fast and are best picked when they are about 8–10in (20–25cm) long and the skin is tender. Harvesting regularly helps to keep the plant producing fruit.

OTHER CLIMBERS

Any crop that puts out tendrils should adapt well to a bicycle trellis. Try planting one or two sugar snap pea plants in a wide container after the last frost, and support them with sticks until they reach the first wheel. They may need some training, so wind them gently around the spokes until they begin to cling. Water them well and protect them from slugs and snails.

Potted bean arch

Easy-to-grow climbing beans reach dizzy heights. Use them to frame a doorway with their pretty flowers, and enjoy a nonstop supply of beans all summer.

Materials

2 x matching containers, at least 3ft (1m) long, 1ft (30cm) wide, and 18in (45cm) deep.
10 x wooden poles or canes, 6–8ft (1.8–2.5m) long.
Multipurpose soil mix

Plastic ties or garden twine
Liquid fertilizer
Watering can

Plants

Borlotti beans:
'Lingua di Fuoco 2'

Green beans:
'Cobra'
'Kentucky Wonder'

Runner beans:
'St. George'
'White Lady'

Try growing green, runner, and Borlotti beans together for a stunning display. Red, pink, and white flowers are followed by yellow, purple, red, and green beans.

2 Insert four poles close to the inside edge of each planter, leaning them toward the center so they cross over each other, forming an arch. Tie them in place with string or ties.

1 Beans do best in a sunny, sheltered location but will also grow in partial shade. Place the containers on each side of a doorway or beside a path, and fill them with soil mix.

Care Advice

Pinch off the growing tips of your beans when they reach the top of the poles to encourage sideshoots.

Keep picking because while there are still flowers on your runner beans there will be more beans to come. Look out for tough old beans hidden among the leaves, and remove them before the plants stop fruiting.

3 Beans often reach 8ft (2.5m) in height and need a strong support. Add a horizontal pole to strengthen the arch, tying it in to the vertical poles where they cross.

4 Tie in a second horizontal pole halfway down the vertical poles to stabilize the arch and create a sturdy structure for these vigorous climbing plants.

5 Sow 2 or 3 beans directly into the soil mix at the base of each pole, after the last frost. If any fail to germinate, resow a few weeks later to give you a succession of beans.

6 Alternatively, start your beans off in pots indoors from mid-spring onward, then harden them off and plant out after the last frost. Tie the plants in to help them climb.

7 Water the plants in well and continue to water regularly, especially when the flowers start to appear. After 4–6 weeks, start feeding weekly with liquid tomato fertilizer.

8 Pick the young, succulent pods every 2–3 days to keep the beans coming. Later in the season, stop picking Borlotti pods and leave the beans to develop for drying.

9 If you have spare space in the containers, sow quick-growing crops, such as arugula, radishes, or mustard greens at the base of your beans. Resow as they mature.

Don't just reuse and recycle...
Reinvent!

All plants need in **order to grow** is **soil mix**, **light**, and **water**, so as long as your **containers and planters** provide these, you can **use almost anything** to grow crops in. **Recycling old objects** is especially rewarding, since it allows you to be **truly creative** and to grow your own **healthy produce** in a **sustainable** way. Here, **reclaimed oil drums**, stacked together, provide a home for herbs, chili peppers, and tomatoes in a small yard.

Pallet planter

With a few adaptations, a wood pallet makes an innovative planter, providing a living wall of crops that is right on trend.

Materials

Recycled wood pallet
Landscape fabric
Multipurpose soil mix

Scissors
Staple gun and staples
Small watering can

Plants

Strawberries
Trailing tomatoes, lettuce
sage, thyme, and marjoram.

Dianthus, violas, and
nasturtiums.
Seeds of your choice

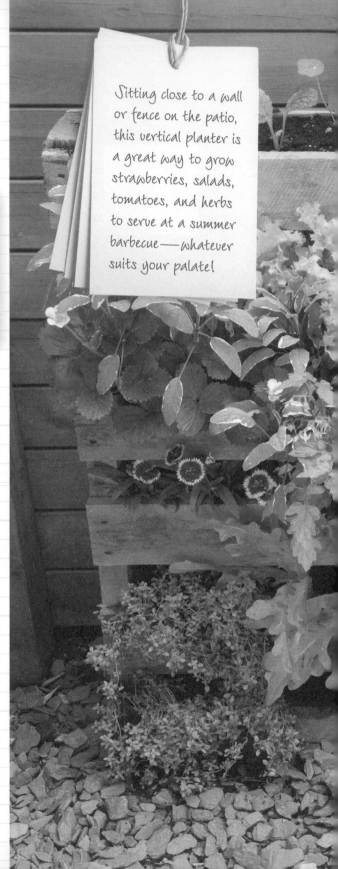

Sitting close to a wall or fence on the patio, this vertical planter is a great way to grow strawberries, salads, tomatoes, and herbs to serve at a summer barbecue—whatever suits your palate!

1 Pallets are usually easy to come by. Try a junk yard or local business for a medium-sized pallet that is undamaged and has roomy slots for plants to colonize.

2 The soil mix is contained in pockets attached to each rung of the pallet. Cut fabric pieces that measure a little more than the length of a section and twice the depth.

3 Use your first piece as a template to cut the rest of the pockets. Each piece is folded along its length to form a pocket, with the ends close against the sides of the pallet.

4 Position the first pocket in the top of the pallet. Ensure the fabric fits snugly at the ends with no gaps for soil mix to fall through.

5 Staple the pocket to one side using a staple gun; then turn the pallet over to attach the second side. Ensure the fabric is secure. It needs to be able to take the weight of the wet soil mix, as well as the plants.

6 Work your way down the rungs, attaching a pocket to the sides of each section to create, in this case, 18 separate growing compartments. Stand the pallet upright.

SOAKING

Moisture is at a premium in confined growing spaces, so before you plant your crops, give them a good soaking. While they are still in their pots, stand them in a tub of water and leave them there until bubbles stop rising from the pots. Remove them and let them drain.

7 Place the pallet in position and secure it safely to the fence or wall before starting to fill the pockets. Fill the top with soil mix, then use a small trowel and your hands to carefully fill the lower compartments.

8 Continue packing soil mix into the pockets to make use of every inch of space. Leave room at the top for watering.

9 Design a plan before you start planting to create an attractive balance of trailing plants, bushy herbs, and flowers. Put trailing plants higher up and shade-tolerant herbs lower down—seeds can be sown in the top.

10 Plant young lettuce plants by tucking them into the slots sideways and pushing the root ball down into the soil mix.

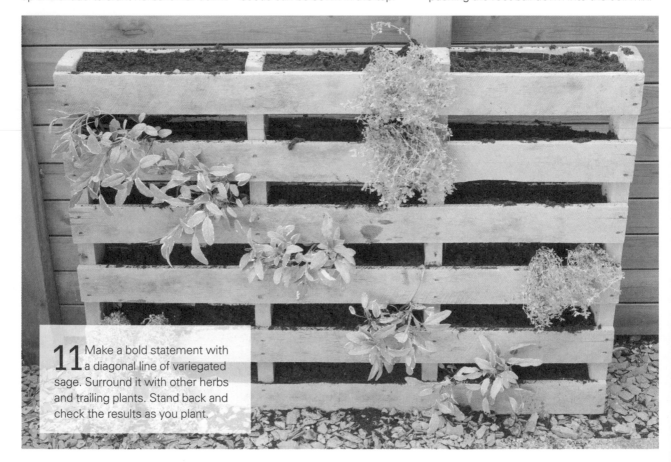

11 Make a bold statement with a diagonal line of variegated sage. Surround it with other herbs and trailing plants. Stand back and check the results as you plant.

13 Use a watering can with a long spout to soak each level of the pallet thoroughly, and pack extra soil mix into any spaces that appear after the soil has settled.

12 When you are happy with the way the side is planted, plant the top with trailing plants, such as trailing tomatoes, strawberries, and nasturtiums. You can also sow seeds of quick-growing crops, like salad leaves and radishes.

Care Advice

Tidy up To keep your pallet looking great, remove weak growth and straggly leaves, harvest crops regularly, and deadhead flowering plants

Harvesting Crop the lettuce by cutting individual greens, leaving the plant to grow. Pinch the leaves from herbs as you need them, and harvest fruit regularly.

14 Keep watering! The slots at the front need particular attention to support a dense colony of plants in such a little space with no chance of rain reaching the soil mix.

Zucchini in a bag

Reusable plastic shopping bags are strong and durable, and are large enough to grow prolific crops, such as zucchini. They are also easy to store in winter.

Materials

Reusable plastic shopping bags
Multipurpose soil mix
Liquid tomato fertilizer
Watering can

Plants and seeds

1 plant per bag (Grow them from seed, sown under cover in mid-spring, or buy them.)

Try 'Goldie' for golden fruit and decorative foliage or 'Defender' for an abundant crop of green fruit. Give your plants room to grow, planting them 3ft (90cm) apart.

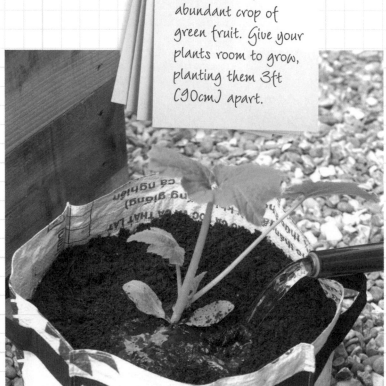

2 Water the plant in and keep it well watered throughout the season, especially during hot spells, to prevent powdery mildew. Once the first flowers appear, feed weekly with liquid tomato fertilizer.

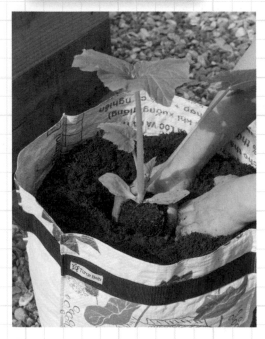

1 Fill the shopping bag with soil mix, leaving room at the top for watering. Plant out small plants, one per bag, when there is no longer a risk of frost, and firm them in.

Care Advice

Sow plants a few weeks apart to avoid gluts and to provide nonstop supplies of this versatile crop all summer long. Zucchini flowers are edible too.

Zucchini will not thrive in cold, wet conditions, so make sure temperatures have really warmed up before you plant them outside.

3 Snip off the fruit when it is young, thin-skinned, and tasty. Keep an eye on the plant since zucchini seem to become oversized as soon as you turn your back!

4 Harvest continually to encourage plants to produce more fruit. Because each plant will produce up to 20 zucchini if fed and watered well, you may only need one.

Grow a sack of spuds

Large bags are ideal for growing early potatoes. Fill a bag one-third full with soil mix, add three tubers, a deep layer of soil mix, two more tubers, then cover with a final deep layer of soil mix. Water the soil well.

Harvest after the plants have flowered and the top growth begins to fade. Dig out a few potatoes at a time with your hands, or cut the sack to release the entire crop.

Blueberry in a pot

Blueberries are ideal for large containers, where they flower and fruit freely, bearing delicious berries. They must have acidic soil, which you can easily provide.

Blueberries are acid-loving plants, and as well as needing lime-free, acidic potting mix, they should also be watered using rainwater. Most tap water is alkaline.

Materials

Large container
at least 18in (45cm) across
Acidic potting mix
Water barrel to collect rainwater
Bamboo poles
Plastic netting

Plants

Blueberry plant
(You may need two.)

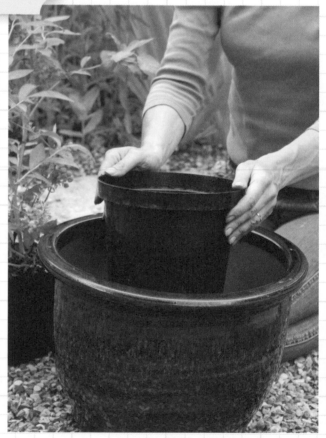

1 Choose a container at least 18in (45cm) wide, ensuring it has drainage holes in the base. Make some if it doesn't. Add acidic potting mix to the bottom of the container.

2 To help avoid disturbing the roots of your plant, slide it from its pot. Place the pot in your container, setting it on soil mix so its top sets 2in (5cm) below the container rim.

4 Turn the pot slightly to loosen it, then lift it out. You will be left with a pot-shaped hole, the ideal size, shape, and depth for your blueberry plant.

3 Fill around the blueberry's old pot with moist soil mix, firming it gently as you do so, until you have filled up to the top of it. This will ensure your plant is planted at the correct depth.

5 Lightly tease the root ball with your fingers to loosen the outermost roots, then place it in the container. Firm it in, then water the plant well.

Pollination

Blueberry flowers must be pollinated before they will set fruit. Some varieties are self-pollinating, meaning you only need one plant. Most are not, so you will need to grow two.

Care Advice

Watering Keep plants moist at all times, watering them with rainwater.

Feeding Blueberries flower and fruit over a long period. As soon as the first blooms appear, start feeding them with a liquid tomato fertilizer each month.

Pruning Plants only need pruning after their second year. In spring, remove any weak, dead, and diseased growth. Prune fruited stems back to healthy buds, and thin out a third of the oldest stems.

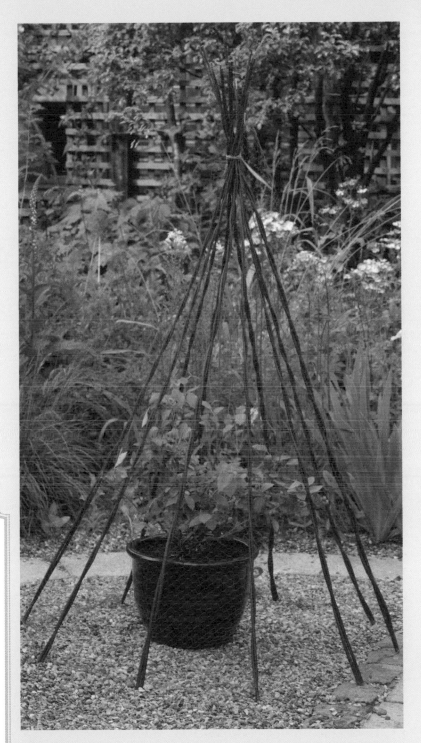

6 Birds love blueberries and will eat them as soon as they start to ripen. Protect plants using fine plastic netting, or make a simple fruit cage.

DIY window box

Why buy when you can make? This simple rustic window box is easy enough for a DIY novice and can be tailor-made to fit the space available.

Materials

Pretreated wood planks, ½in (1.5cm) thick
Tape measure
Pencil
Wood saw
Power drill with wood bits

Screws—1½in (4cm) long
Screwdriver
Copper tape
Galvanized tacks
Sandpaper
Multipurpose soil mix

Strong winds and visiting birds can dislodge a window box with disastrous results. If you're siting your box on a higher windowsill, make sure that it is properly secured.

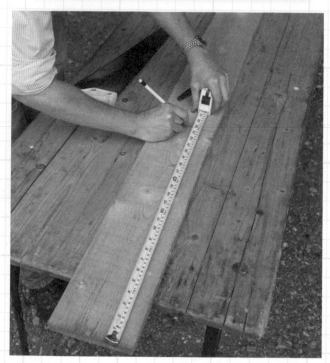

1 Make sure your windowsill is level and able to support a box before measuring it to decide on the length and depth of your window box. Two small boxes may be more practical than a long one. Measure and mark the lumber.

2 Lay the wood on a firm surface to support it while you cut the lengths you need. Hold the pieces together to ensure you have cut and measured them accurately.

3 Drill two pilot holes, about ¼in (6mm) in toward the ends of each long side of the box—these will help to keep the wood from splitting. Then screw the sides together to form a neat rectangle.

HANDY HERBS

Any cook would welcome a bed
of mixed fragrant herbs growing
just outside a window—much
cheaper and fresher than store-
bought herb packs and pots.

Care Advice

Maintenance If you like, you can paint your box inside and out with wood preservative to protect it from water and weather, and prolong its life.

Plants Pinch off the tops of herb plants to encourage bushy growth. Introduce a few small lettuce plants for a handy crop of salad leaves just outside your window.

4 Keeping the box square, screw the sides of the box together. If it wobbles or looks crooked, loosen the screws and readjust the joints. Then tighten all the screws.

5 When all four sides have been joined together, insert the base and hold it in place firmly. First, drill pilot holes, then screw through the sides into the base to secure it.

6 Screw small wood pieces across the base of the box to create feet. This allows water to drain easily and raises the base off the wet sill, helping to prevent wood decay.

7 Use a large drill bit to drill holes at regular intervals through the base of the box to provide good drainage and prevent plants from becoming waterlogged.

9 Secure the tape by tapping in galvanized tacks, spaced evenly to create an attractive, rustic finish. Sand the box lightly to remove splinters and smooth the edges.

8 To deter slugs and snails, stick a band of copper tape around the outside of the window box, keeping it level. A static charge from the copper repels the pests.

10 Fill the box almost to the top with soil mix, allowing space for watering, and plant it with your chosen plants. Water well and place the box on the windowsill.

Squash trellis

Beautifully decorative and a great use of vertical space, training squash up a trellis is a wonderful way to grow this vegetable in confined areas.

Materials

Large metal container
Bubble wrap
Multipurpose soil mix
Wooden poles or canes
Soft string

Scissors
Liquid fertilizer
Mulch
Watering can

Plants

Squash plants
Nasturtiums (optional)

Squash come in an exciting array of shapes and sizes, and can be easily grown from seed. Try acorn-shaped 'Mini Red Turban' or the trombonelike 'Tromboncino'.

2 Ensure each side of the metal container is insulated, then make small holes in the bubble wrap to allow water to drain freely. The container can then be placed in a sunny location and filled with multipurpose soil mix.

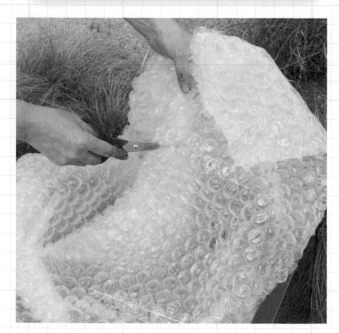

1 Metal containers look attractive but can heat up quickly in hot weather. To keep the roots of your plants cool, insulate the container inside using plastic bubble wrap.

Growing Advice

Watering and feeding Water plants well, especially in hot, dry spells, ensuring the potting mix never dries out. After 4–6 weeks, feed weekly with a liquid fertilizer to ensure a good harvest.

Training As the squash plants grow, tie their stems carefully to the trellis with string, covering it evenly.

4 Once the risk of frost has passed, plant your squash, ensuring they are hardened off first. For smaller varieties, plant two plants per container, 12–18in (30–45cm) apart.

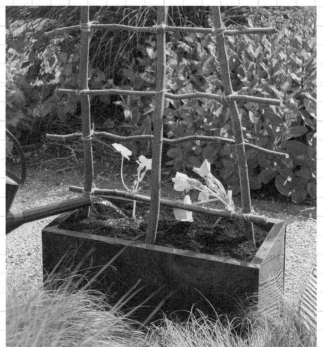

3 Insert tall wooden or bamboo poles upright into the container, then attach shorter laterals using string to create an open framework. Ensure it is sturdy and secure.

5 Water the plants in well and start training them vertically by tying their stems to the framework using soft string. Train them regularly to ensure they can support their fruit.

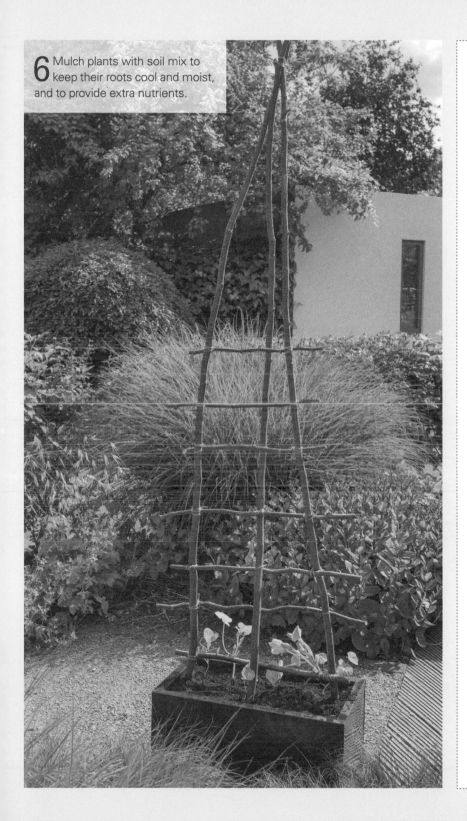

6 Mulch plants with soil mix to keep their roots cool and moist, and to provide extra nutrients.

Useful tips

Promote ripening
Snip off or move aside any leaves that cast shade on the fruit to help them ripen fully.

Bonus crop In larger containers, plant nasturtiums alongside your squash, and enjoy their edible flowers.

You may lack space but not...
Great ideas!

In order to **make the most** of a small yard, consider **every possible area** where you could **grow crops**, no matter **how unlikely**, then decide **how to use it**. Most crops are **versatile** and **easy to grow**, especially annual ones, which means you can be **really inventive** in **how and where** you grow them. If, for example, you have a **patio table** that's only **used occasionally**, why not use part of it for a crop of **salad greens**?

Growing gutters

Easy to attach to any sunny, vertical surface, plastic gutters are ideal for growing super fast, feather-light crops such as microgreens and pea shoots.

Greens picked while young have a flavor that is more intense than fully grown greens. This is a great way to grow crops such as arugula that tend to bolt when they mature.

Materials and tools

Plastic gutters	Screws
Gutter ends	Screwdriver
Gutter brackets	Power drill
Pencil	Epoxy resin glue
Hacksaw	Multipurpose soil mix
Drill	Watering can

Seeds

Peas
Microgreens—mustard greens, mizuna, arugula
Herbs – basil, fennel, coriander, parsley

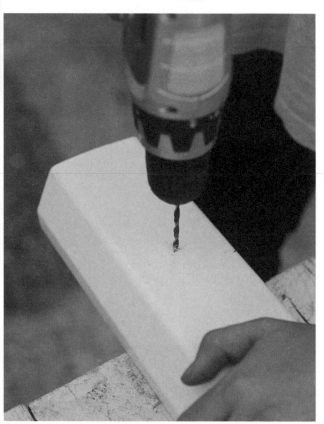

1 Measure your space and decide on the lengths and arrangement of your gutters. Mark the gutter with a pencil and cut the lengths using a hacksaw.

2 Hold the gutter firmly on a solid surface and use a power drill to make drainage holes in the base, spaced about 6in (15cm) apart along its length.

HARVESTING
BABY GREENS

Sited in sun or part-shade, gutters provide the ultimate economical growing space for the impatient gardener. Start harvesting microgreens and herbs within days, and resow the gutters up to three times for fresh or different crops. Then clear out the depleted soil mix, refill the gutters with fresh potting mix, and begin again.

Care Advice

Watering To keep your gutters growing, water them gently but thoroughly every day.

Pests and diseases Microgreens grow fast and are harvested quickly, leaving little time for attack from pests and diseases. Slugs and snails will climb to the feast, so be vigilant and catch them on the way.

3 White gutters are easy to paint to match your garden color scheme. Use simple slide-on ends to keep the soil mix and water in, and glue them in place if need be.

4 Mark positions for the brackets, making sure the gutter is supported in the middle and is level. Drill holes, screw in the brackets, and simply slide the gutters into place.

5 Fill the gutter with soil mix, leaving a small space below the rim for watering. Level it off and firm it gently. Your growing gutter is now ready for sowing seeds.

7 Check your plants within a few days to see if they have germinated. Thin out overcrowded seedlings, eating the thinnings, and leave the rest to grow until ready to pick.

6 Sow seeds fairly densely—every shoot is part of the crop. (*Peas are shown here.*) Cover them lightly with soil mix and water in using a can with a fine nozzle.

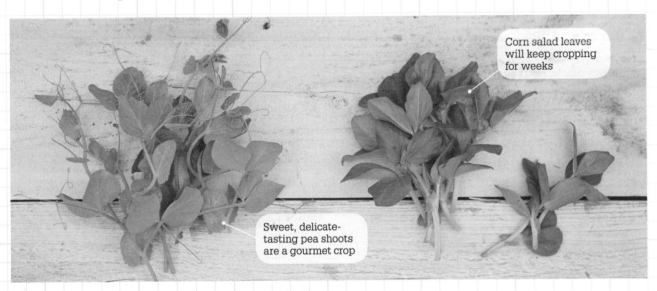

Corn salad leaves will keep cropping for weeks

Sweet, delicate-tasting pea shoots are a gourmet crop

8 Harvest within a week, depending on the crop. Pull microgreens out of the soil, including roots, and wash well before eating. Pick pea shoots and salad greens when they are young and tender.

Productive paving

Herbs can bring your new paths and patios to life.
Plant creeping and flowering herbs between the
pavers for food and fragrance at your feet.

Materials

Paving slabs
Gravel
Landscape fabric
Trowel
Watering can

Plants

Creeping and flowering
herbs, such as chamomile,
Corsican mint, oregano, and
variegated thyme.

Most herbs prefer
a sunny spot and
are easy to care for.
Plant a mix of
flowering herbs, such
as chamomile, and
those with colorful
foliage, such as
variegated thyme.

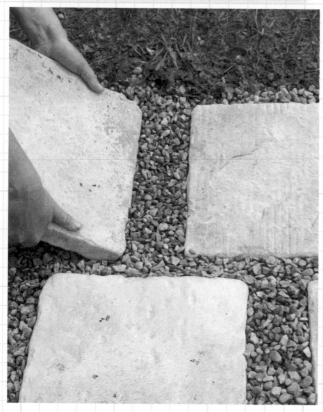

2 Scoop out some gravel between slabs, cut slits in the
fabric beneath, and dig small holes in the soil. Plant the
herbs, and replace the fabric and gravel around their bases.

1 Decide where your new patio or path will be, level the
soil, and lay the landscape fabric. Cover the fabric with
gravel and set your slabs into it, leaving small planting gaps.

3 Water the herbs in well, and keep them moist until they
show signs of new growth. Pinch off their growing tips
to encourage new sideshoots, and trim back excess growth.

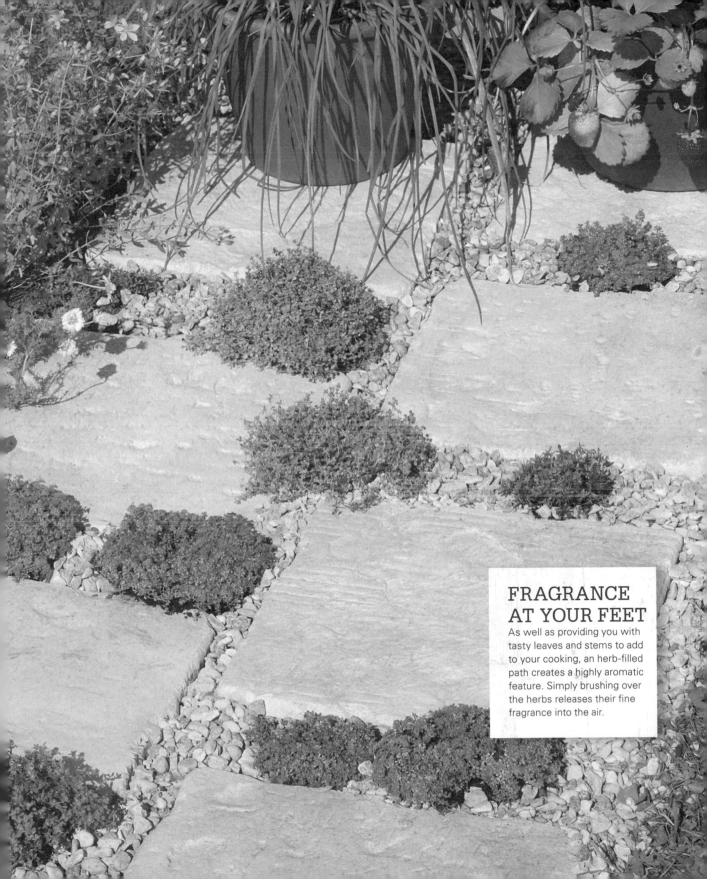

FRAGRANCE AT YOUR FEET

As well as providing you with tasty leaves and stems to add to your cooking, an herb-filled path creates a highly aromatic feature. Simply brushing over the herbs releases their fine fragrance into the air.

Hanging herbs

Many herbs prefer dry, hungry soil, and so thrive in hanging baskets. Position one near your kitchen window or door, and enjoy tasty herbs close at hand.

Materials

Hanging basket
Bracket
Multipurpose soil mix
Trowel
Watering can

Plants

Golden oregano
Purple sage
Curry plant
Chives
Mint
Herbs of your choice

Choose bushy and trailing herbs for an attractive effect, and pick silver-, gold-, and purple-leaf types for visual impact. Hang the basket in a sheltered, sunny location.

1 If you don't already have one, fix a hanging basket bracket at your chosen location. Fill the base of the basket with multipurpose soil mix, leaving space to plant the herbs.

2 Plant the herbs 2in (5cm) below the rim, with trailing types at the edges, bushier ones in the middle or at the back. Fill around them with more soil mix and firm them in.

3 Water the basket well, leave it to drain, then add more soil mix between the plants if required. Attach the chains to the basket and hang it to give the best display.

KEEP YOUR HERBS HAPPY

Water plants regularly to
encourage tender growth, but
feed them just once a month
with balanced liquid fertilizer.
Pinch off the tips to promote
bushiness, and pick the leaves
and stems as you need them.
Evergreen herbs, such as sage
and rosemary, will give color
throughout the winter months.

Wall pockets

Wall-mounted planting pockets are now widely available, and are ideal for growing small crops on sunny vertical surfaces.

Materials

Wall pockets
Multipurpose soil mix
Plastic ties and wire

Bamboo poles
(painted black - optional)
Water-retaining beads

Plants and seeds

Thyme plants
Rosemary plants
Sage plants
Viola plants

Chive plants
Strawberry plants
Microgreen seeds

Wall pockets are well suited to small annual crops and herbs, and there are many designs you can use. In fall they can easily be taken down and stored until the following spring.

1 Decide how much space you want to cover and buy enough planting pockets. Choose a design that suits the space and the plants you want to grow.

2 To keep from drilling multiple holes in your walls, the pockets are hung from a bamboo pole. Fix sturdy wires to hang the poles from.

3 Link the planting pockets together using strong plastic ties. If your pockets don't already have mounting holes, carefully make some, ensuring they cannot easily rip.

4 Join as many pockets together as your pole and wire will safely hold—remember that wet soil mix is heavy. You could also mount them using a small stake and rope.

5 Attach the pole to the uppermost pockets using plastic ties. Fix a pair of level screws to the wall, then hang the pockets, using the mounting wires tied to the pole in step 2.

6 The pockets will quickly dry out once planted, so to help retain moisture, add some water-retaining gel beads to the soil mix. Water the mix before starting to plant.

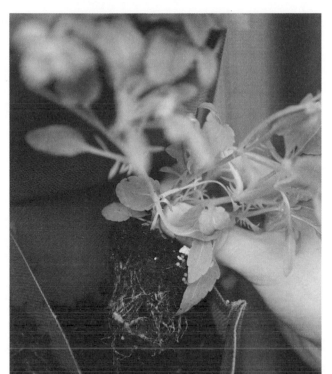

7 Starting from the uppermost pockets, plant them up, leaving about a 2in (5cm) gap below the rim for watering.

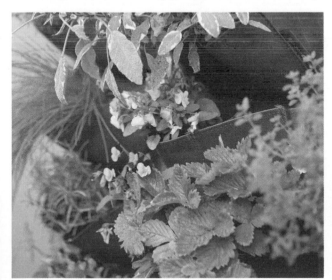

8 Create a display of bushy and trailing plants, and crops grown for their leaves, flowers, and fruits. You can even include small specimens of shrubby herbs, such as sage.

Care Advice

Watering Keep the pockets well watered, checking them every day in warm spells. Water carefully early in the morning, using a watering can with a fine nozzle.

Training Trim back plants that become tangled or look untidy. Deadhead and harvest the crops regularly.

CROPS IN
SMALL YARDS

A nine-pot plot

If you don't have room for a conventional raised bed, you can create a similar amount of growing space by using large containers. Here, nine pots give the same space as a 3x3ft (1x1m) bed, and provide two abundant crops that last from spring to winter.

To **get the most** from your pots, **sow crops** to **harvest** in spring and summer, **doubling** the number of **vegetables** you can **grow** in **one year**. Use the **largest** containers you have **room for**, and **ensure** they have ample **drainage** holes.

You will need

• Materials
Large containers
Multipurpose soil mix
Bamboo poles
Garden string

• Tools
Trowel
Scissors

CROPS—WHEN TO PLANT

Radishes
Sow from mid-spring

Lettuce
Sow from mid-spring

Snow peas
Sow in early spring

Green onions
Sow from late spring

Pea shoots
Sow batches in early spring

Sugar snap peas
Sow in early spring

Carrots
Sow from mid-spring

Beets
Sow from mid-spring

Kale
Sow from mid-spring

Green beans
Sow in early summer

Runner beans
Sow in early summer

Black leaf kale
Sow in spring in small pots

Chinese broccoli
Sow in early summer

Cucumbers
Plant small plants in early summer

Tomatoes
Plant out small plants in early summer

African basil
Plant out in early summer

Chili peppers
Plant small plants outside in early summer

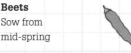
French tarragon
Plant in early summer

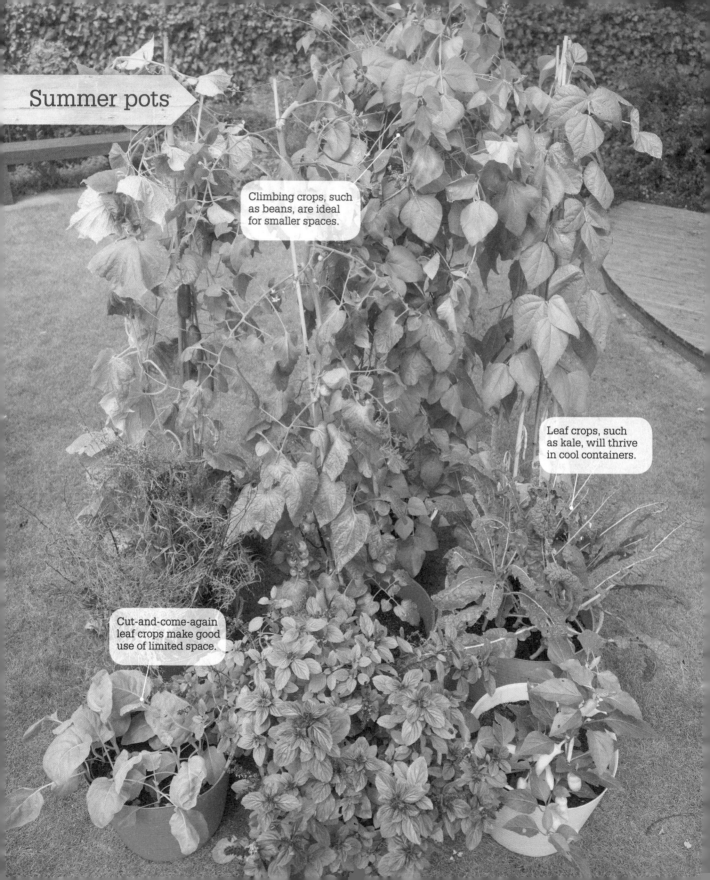

Summer pots

Climbing crops, such as beans, are ideal for smaller spaces.

Leaf crops, such as kale, will thrive in cool containers.

Cut-and-come-again leaf crops make good use of limited space.

Alternative crops to grow

Spring

Arugula
Instead of green onions This peppery-tasting leaf crop can be sown directly into a container during spring.

Mustard greens
Instead of radishes Grow as a cut-and-come-again salad. Sow the seeds directly in the container, then thin the plants.

Swiss chard
Instead of kale Sow seeds directly into the container or plant small plants. This crop will last into winter if left to continue growing.

Summer squash
Instead of peas or beans Train the plants up bamboo tepees to make best use of small spaces. Water and feed the plants well.

Spinach
Instead of Chinese Broccoli Sow seeds into the container. Pick individual leaves or cut whole plants, allowing them to regrow.

Kohlrabi
Instead of kale This unusual-looking vegetable is grown for its plump, tender stems. Sow seed in early summer.

Summer

Asian greens
Instead of French tarragon This is a quick-growing leaf crop that can be resown repeatedly in summer, every 3–4 weeks.

Basil
Instead of African basil If you cannot find the African plants, this annual type can be sown directly in early summer.

Zucchini
Instead of peas or beans These large plants need plenty of water and fertilizer. Plant in early summer and enjoy the bounty.

Pot 1 Spring

Radishes are one of the quickest crops you can grow, and are ready to harvest in 4–6 weeks. Sow seeds directly in spring and harvest in early summer.

1 Radishes grow quickly, so thin them out as soon as seedlings are large enough to handle to keep the plants healthy.

2 Keep the plants well watered and pull the roots once they reach a usable size. Pull some as baby roots, others once full size.

Pot 1 Summer

Green beans can be started once the radishes are pulled. Add slow-release fertilizer to the soil mix and insert tall poles, tied into a tepee, for support.

1 Seed can be sown in late spring under cover, ready to plant out. They can also be sown directly at the base of each stake, once the radishes are removed.

2 Position in a sheltered, sunny site, and water well. Feed weekly with liquid tomato fertilizer once the first flowers appear. Harvest the beans regularly to keep them coming through the fall.

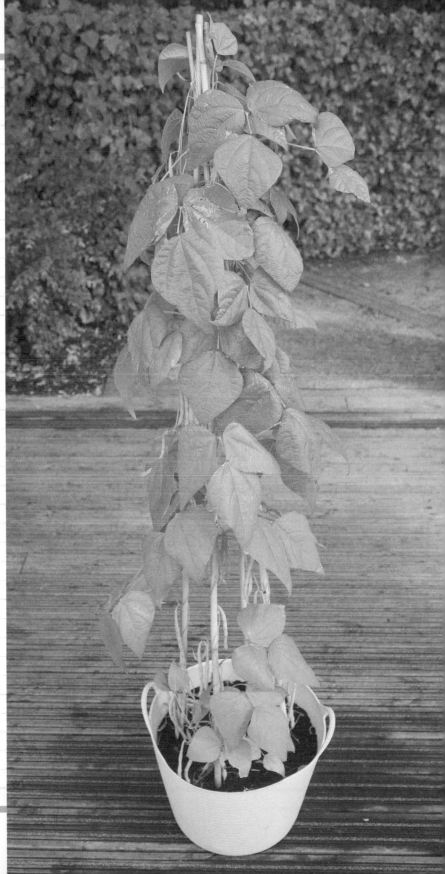

Pot 2 Spring

Lettuce is quick and easy to grow. It can be harvested as baby leaves as soon as it is large enough, or as full-size heads after 9–12 weeks.

1 Sow the seeds thinly on the surface in spring. As the seedlings grow, thin them out, using the thinnings as a crop of baby greens. Leave four plants to form heads.

2 Harvest the heads once large enough in early summer, or pick the outer leaves individually as and when you need them.

Pot 2 Summer

Runner beans crop well in pots if well watered. Young plants can be raised under cover in late spring to plant out, or sow the seeds directly in early summer.

1 Provide a tall support, tie in new growth, and keep the plants well watered. Once the first flowers appear, start feeding plants weekly with a liquid tomato fertilizer.

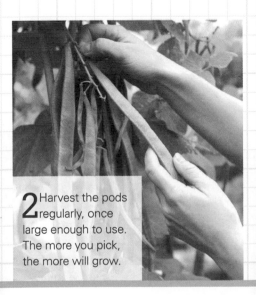

2 Harvest the pods regularly, once large enough to use. The more you pick, the more will grow.

Pot 3 Spring

Snow peas taste delicious, and although they are expensive to buy, they are very easy to grow. The seeds are sown directly in the container in spring.

1 All peas need something to cling onto when growing, so insert some twigs or sticks into the potting mix for support.

2 Keep plants well watered, especially once in flower. Pick the pods whole just as the peas inside begin to form.

Pot 3 Summer

Black leaf kale is a type of kale grown for its rich-tasting leaves. It is slow-growing but can be picked as young or mature leaves from late summer until spring.

1 Sow seed in small pots in spring, thin out the seedlings to one per pot, and grow them until the peas are harvested. They can then be planted into the container.

2 Water the plants well and provide taller plants with support. Harvest the outer leaves once large enough.

Pot 4 Spring

Green onions are grown for their leaves and bulbs, which give a mild onion-flavored crunch to salads. Red varieties give a welcome splash of color.

1 Sow seed directly in the container during spring, and thin the seedlings to 1in (2.5cm) apart so they will reach a good size.

2 Keep the green onions well watered, and pull the plants whole once the stems are pencil-thick. Loosen the soil mix if needed.

HARVESTING
If you pull the individual green onions carefully when harvesting, smaller plants can be left to keep growing, making full use of the crop. Use pickings like chives.

Pot 4 Summer

Chinese broccoli, which is also know as kai lan, is grown for its succulent leaves, shoots, and flowers. Sown in spring, it is ready to harvest in 8–10 weeks.

1 Sow seeds directly in the container and thin seedlings to 8in (20cm) apart. Keep them well watered, and check plants for caterpillars (*above*), which attack them.

2 When the stems reach 8–10in (20–25cm) tall, cut them back to 3in (7.5cm) high. Leave the plants to grow back, then harvest them again later.

Pot 5 Spring

Pea shoots are fantastically quick to grow and are ready to harvest in about three weeks. The plants can be harvested two or three times during spring.

1 Soak the seeds overnight and sow them directly in the container, 1in (2.5cm) apart. You can use any pea seeds for pea shoots.

2 When shoots are 4–6in (10–15cm) tall, cut them just above the lowest leaves. Keep them well watered and they will regrow, giving 2–3 more crops.

WATER WELL

Pea shoots should be kept moist at all times to ensure they taste their best. Regular watering also helps to keep powdery mildew away from the plants (*see p.245*).

Pot 5 Summer

Cucumbers need a warm, sheltered site, and a tall support to climb. Varieties with smaller fruit are the most productive, especially when harvested often.

1 Plant out small cucumber plants once the risk of frost has passed and the peas have been removed. Tie in their stems to the support at first.

2 Keep plants moist and feed weekly with liquid tomato fertilizer once the first flowers appear. Harvest the fruit when they reach a usable size.

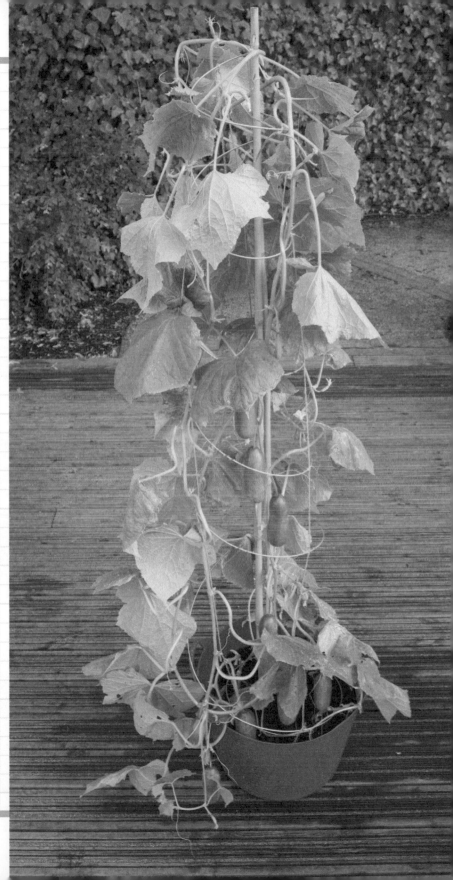

Pot 6 Spring

Sugar snap peas produce sweet-tasting pods from late spring. They are easy to grow from seeds sown directly in the container in early spring.

1 Peas need support, so insert 3–4 twiggy stems into the container before sowing the seeds. Tie in the young stems, after which they will climb naturally. Keep the plants well watered.

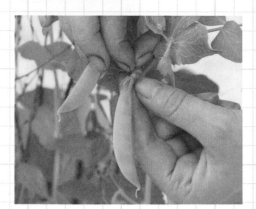

2 Pick the pods when round and plump, but before the peas inside are firm. Harvest regularly to encourage cropping.

Pot 6 Summer

Tomatoes need a sheltered, warm site. Cordon varieties, grown as a single stem, are best for containers. There are many fascinating varieties to try.

1 Plant out a young plant in early summer, and insert a 6ft (2m) pole to support its single stem. Keep plants well watered and tie the stem to the pole as it grows.

2 Remove any sideshoots that form from the main stem. Feed plants weekly with tomato fertilizer after the first flowers appear. Harvest the fruit when they pull easily from the vine—pick often.

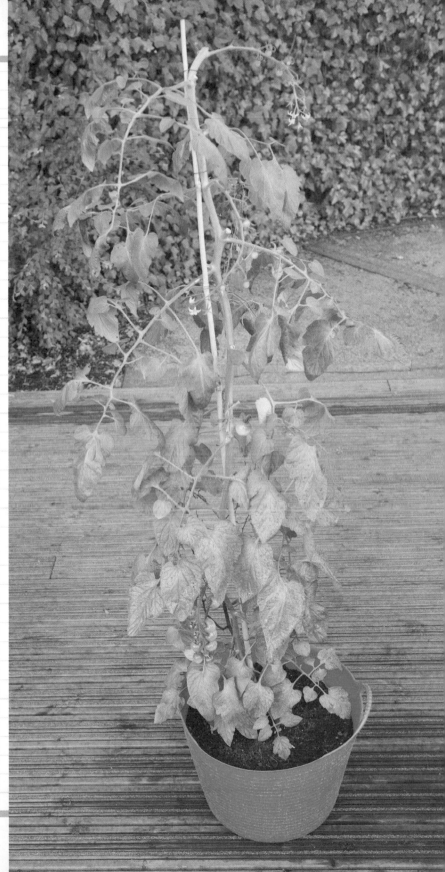

Pot 7 Spring

Carrots are sweet and tender when harvested young, and are ready to pull after 12 weeks. Early varieties tend to be short or round-rooted, so ideal for pots.

1 Sow seed thinly to avoid attracting carrot rust flies (*see p.242*). These pests are attracted by the carrot scent.

2 Keep the plants well watered and pull the roots when they reach a usable size. Take care not to disturb any that are still growing.

SCENT TRAIL

To help prevent carrot rust flies from finding your crop, place it near strongly scented plants, such as African basil. The scent will mask the telltale carrot aroma.

Pot 7 Summer

African basil is a tender perennial with richly aromatic purple-tinted foliage. Like basil, the leaves are great for salads, pestos, and sauces.

1 Only available as plants, plant one into your container in early summer once the risk of frost has passed. Place it in full sun, and water and feed it regularly.

2 Pinch off the tips to encourage sideshoots, and pick the leaves and stems all summer. Bring the plant under cover for winter.

Pot 8 Spring

Beets can be ready to pull in as little as eight weeks, when the roots are sweet and tender. The leaves can also be lightly picked, and used like Swiss chard.

MICRO BEETS
Although beets are usually grown for their plump roots, you can also grow them as a micro crop. Pull after 2–3 weeks and eat the leaves, stems, and tiny roots.

1 Sow seeds directly in the container and thin the seedlings to 2–4in (5–10cm) apart. You can add the thinnings to salads.

2 Keep the plants well watered to ensure the roots are tender, and harvest them as soon as they are large enough to use.

Pot 8 Summer

Chili peppers come in a dazzling array of shapes, sizes, and colors. When growing outdoors, give them a sheltered, warm site to crop at their best.

1 Peppers need a long growing season, so start seeds off indoors in early spring, or buy small plants. Plant out hardened-off plants after the last frost in early summer.

2 Water the plants regularly, and feed them weekly with liquid tomato fertilizer once the first flowers appear. The fruit can be harvested when green and milder in taste, or when fully ripe and hot.

Pot 9 Spring

Kale is usually grown as a winter crop (*see p.141*), but if sown in early spring, the outer leaves can also be harvested repeatedly until early summer.

1 Sow seeds under cover in pots during late winter, harden off the seedlings, and plant them into the container in early spring.

2 Once the plants are large enough, start using the older outer leaves, leaving the young inner ones to continue growing.

Pot 9 Summer

French tarragon is a delicious, half-hardy herb that benefits from being grown in a container. Use the leaves in chicken and fish dishes, or in soups and salads.

1 Best bought as young plants in early summer, plant them into the container once the risk of frost has passed. Pinch off the tops of the stems for bushier plants.

2 Keep the plants moist and feed regularly with a balanced liquid fertilizer. The leaves and stems can be picked as needed. Bring the plant indoors in winter.

Yield Spring

Crops sown early spring will give a bountiful harvest at the end of the season. Many can be picked over several weeks.

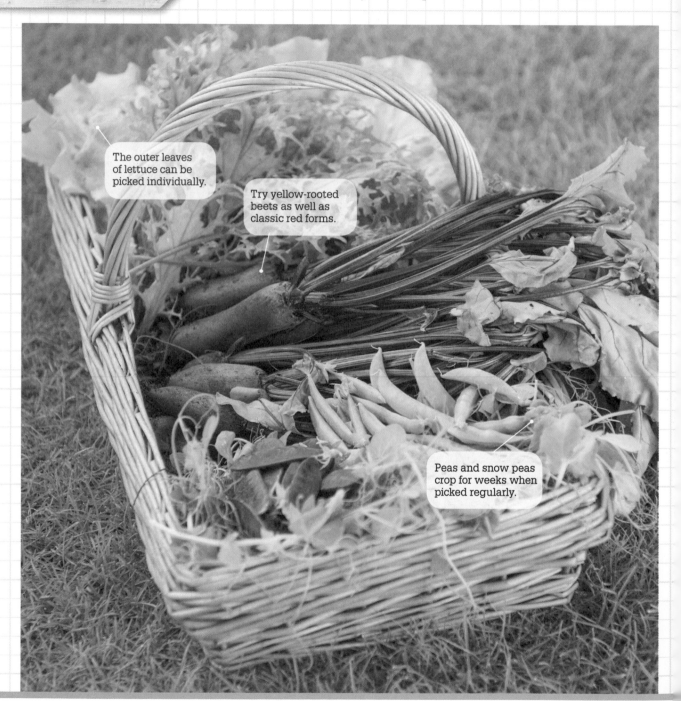

The outer leaves of lettuce can be picked individually.

Try yellow-rooted beets as well as classic red forms.

Peas and snow peas crop for weeks when picked regularly.

Yield Summer

Most summer crops can be harvested over many weeks, rewarding your efforts with ample fresh and tasty produce.

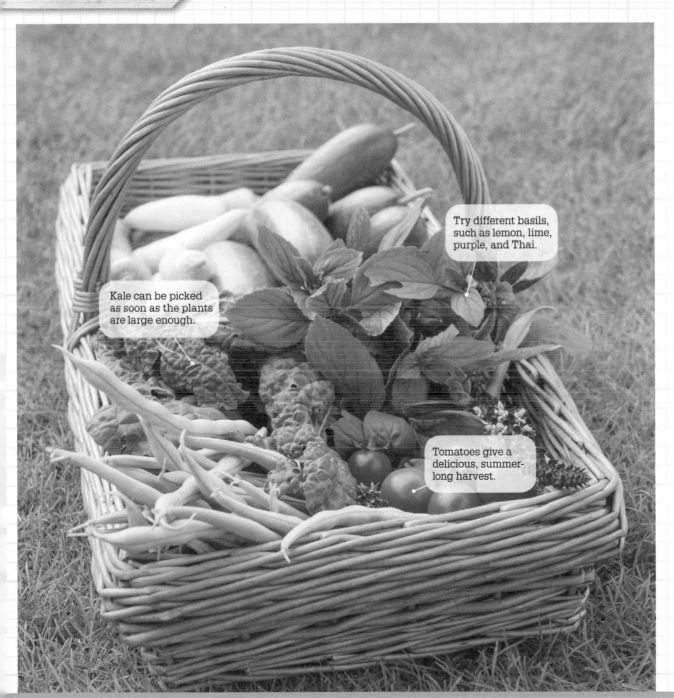

Where space allows use...
Raised beds

There are **many advantages** to growing your crops in a **raised bed** (*see pp.20–23*), but as well as providing ideal **growing conditions**, they can also make an **attractive feature**. When choosing what to grow, consider varieties with **positive qualities**, such as **colorful foliage** or **flowers**, and **combine crops** with different leaf **textures**. Rather than **planting in rows**, why not arrange your crops in **interesting patterns** instead?

DIY raised bed

Sunny walls provide warmth and shelter, encouraging plants to grow. It's the ideal place to position a three-sided raised bed, which you can easily make yourself.

You will need

- **Materials**
Pretreated wood planks at least 2in (5cm) thick
Long wood screws
Scrap wood pieces
Plastic sheeting

Topsoil, potting mix, and grit

- **Tools**
Power drill, saw, tape measure, and a shovel.

Raised beds can be made from many different materials. Wood is ideal, since it is easy to use, and when treated with preservative, it can be very long-lasting.

1 The bed consists of a three-sided wood frame placed against a wall to form a box. Decide how large you want your bed to be, then measure, mark, and saw the pieces of wood to length on a firm, level surface.

2 Depending on how high you want your bed to be, join the first three sides at the corners to form a frame. Drill pilot holes, then attach the sides, using long screws. Repeat, if you are making a deeper bed, using two or more frames.

3 Choose a level site and place the first frame in position against the wall. Place your second, and even third, frame on top. Make certain that each added frame sets squarely on the one below it.

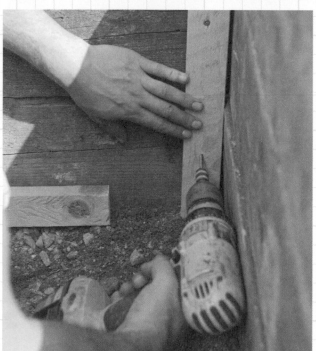

4 With all the frames in place and squared up, cut wood pieces, two per side, to connect them together. Drill pilot holes, then screw the wood in place.

5 Cut plastic sheeting and a piece of wood the full length of the bed. Screw the wood to the wall, through the lower edge of the plastic sheeting, to hold it in place.

6 Fold the first piece of plastic sheeting down and into the bed, so that it covers the wall. This will keep the wall from getting damp. Now, cut more plastic sheeting to fully line the inside of the bed and nail it in place. This will protect the wood from decay and help to retain moisture.

OPTIONAL EXTRA

To take full advantage of the warmth and shelter provided by a sunny wall, consider installing a trellis before positioning the bed. This will allow you to grow climbing crops, including heat-loving melons or beans. Alternatively, rather than a trellis, you could also attach horizontal wires to the wall. Wires are more flexible than a trellis, and are ideal for training fruiting crops, such as raspberries and Japanese wineberries.

8 Fill the bed with a mixture of topsoil, soil mix, and grit (*see p.23*), mixing it in a wheelbarrow first. Water the mix, allow to settle for a few days, then top it off if needed.

Care Advice

Wood care Even pretreated wood benefits from being painted with wood preservative each year. This is best done in fall, when the bed is likely to be empty. Use a wood preservative harmless to plants.

7 If the bed is more than 36in (90cm) deep, place some gravel in the bottom to ensure good drainage.

The easy-to-grow bed

Planted with crops that are quick and easy to grow, this bed will supply you with an abundance of colorful, nourishing, tasty leaves and fruit from spring to winter.

When **planting** your bed, be aware that **strawberry plants** are perennial and take up **permanent space**. Use the space around them for **quick-growing** crops. **Sow** new batches of **seeds** as soon as **space is available**, and always sow a **few extras** in case of **slug** and **snail** damage. **Surplus** plants can be **thinned**.

Spring

GETTING STARTED Plant the strawberries, which will remain in the bed all year. Sow the seeds of your spring crops directly in the soil, ready to harvest a few weeks later.

You will need

- **Materials**
Raised bed, approximately 3ft (1m) square
Potting mix, soil, and grit
Bamboo poles
Fine plastic netting

- **Tools**
Spade
Trowel
Watering can
String guides

Summer

Fall

GETTING AHEAD Remove the spring crops, plant out the tomato plants, and sow your summer crops. Sow Swiss chard and mustard greens in pots to plant out in fall.

EXTENDING THE SEASON Leave the strawberries where they are but remove all other summer crops. Plant out the Swiss chard and mustard greens sown in pots in summer.

CROPS—WHEN TO SOW OR PLANT

Peas
Sow direct in
early spring.

Green onions
Sow in batches
in early spring.

Lettuce
Sow in spring.

Strawberries
Plant out in
early spring.

Nasturtiums
Sow seeds in
mid-spring.

Pea shoots
Sow in batches
during summer.

Swiss chard
Sow in summer
into small pots.

Mustard greens
Sow in summer
into small pots.

Tomatoes
Sow seeds in
mid-spring.

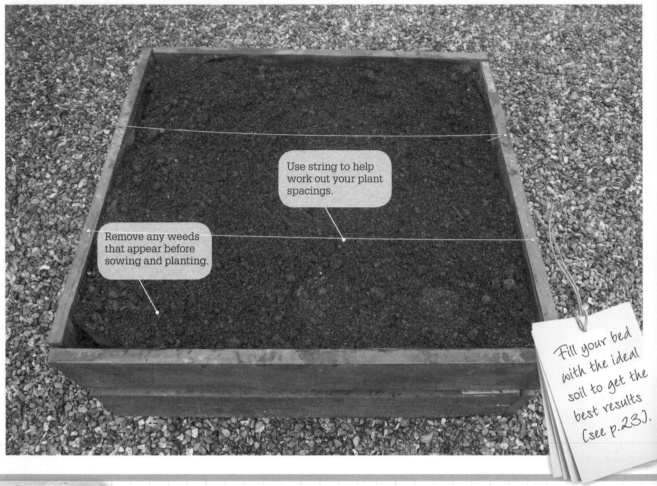

Use string to help work out your plant spacings.

Remove any weeds that appear before sowing and planting.

Fill your bed with the ideal soil to get the best results (see p.23).

Spring

Now is the time to start sowing the first seeds and planting strawberries. To give your crops a useful head start, warm the soil first (*see pp.44–45*).

1 Strawberry plants need time to establish, so plant them first. You can then sow your annual crops in the remainder of the bed around them.

2 Once the soil is warm enough, sow your seeds into shallow furrows, to the depth and spacing recommended on the packet. Water them in gently.

SOW UNDER COVER

If the weather is cold, start your seeds off under cover, ready to plant out in a few weeks. Peas can even be started in old rain gutters.

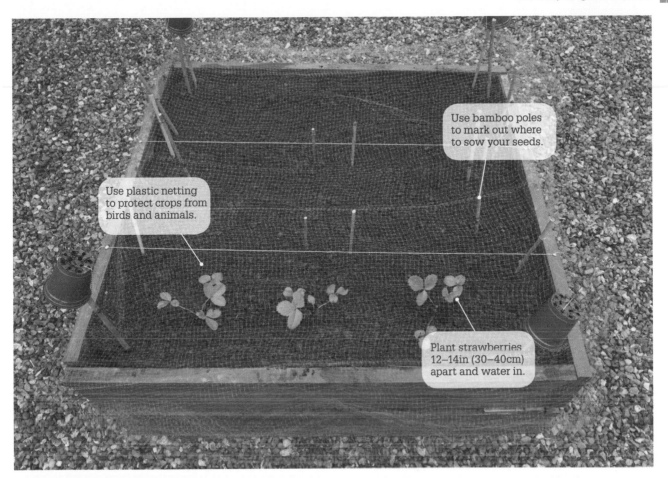

Use bamboo poles to mark out where to sow your seeds.

Use plastic netting to protect crops from birds and animals.

Plant strawberries 12–14in (30–40cm) apart and water in.

3 Snip off strawberry runners, the long stems with young plants attached, so the plants put all their energy into producing berries.

4 Thin out your vegetable seedlings as they grow, leaving the strongest ones at the recommended planting distances (*see pp.32–34*).

5 Don't waste the thinnings, the surplus seedlings removed during thinning. Many, such as lettuce, can be harvested as baby vegetables.

Spring

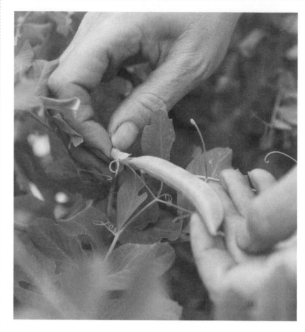

Sugar snap peas can be harvested and eaten whole, as soon as the juvenile peas start to swell within the pods. Wait until the pods have plumped up slightly, and eat them on the day they are picked for the best flavor.

GROWING GREEN ONIONS

Weed around green onions, being careful of their shallow roots, so that they don't have competition for nutrients and water. Sow batches every few weeks from spring to summer for a constant supply. If you have enough space, you could also continue sowing throughout summer.

GENERAL CARE

DON'T FORGET TO:
- Keep all plants well watered
- Weed between plants carefully
- Regularly check for signs of pests
- Pick fruiting crops regularly
- Deadhead flowering plants
- Resow new batches of seed
- Ensure nets are securely fastened

SPRING LETTUCE Crop lettuce by picking the outer leaves, rather than pulling up the whole plant, and leave the inner ones to continue growing. Alternatively, cut the head off near the base, leaving the stump to resprout.

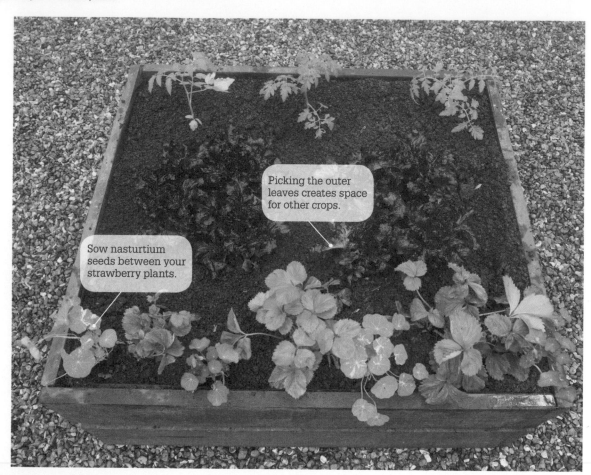

Picking the outer leaves creates space for other crops.

Sow nasturtium seeds between your strawberry plants.

Summer

Once the peas have been harvested, remove the plants and replace them with young tomatoes. Continue to harvest the outer lettuce leaves.

1 Harvest the green onions by pulling them from the soil. Prepare the area for resowing by removing any plant debris, and lightly turning the soil.

2 Sow a new batch of green onions, or another quick-growing crop, such as pea shoots. These too can soon be replaced, once harvested.

3 Water your tomato plants regularly, especially in drier weather. Erratic watering when the fruit start to form can cause them to split and spoil.

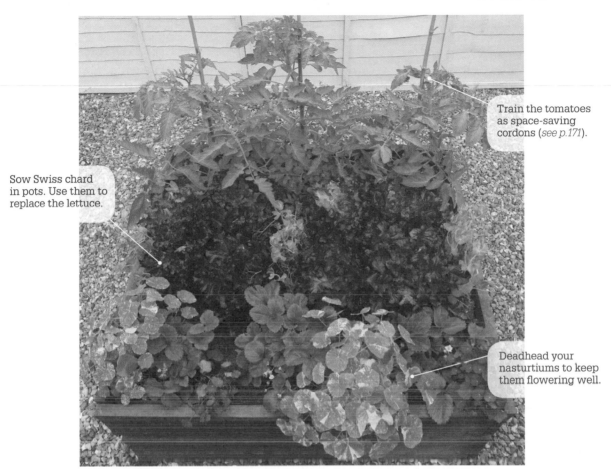

Sow Swiss chard in pots. Use them to replace the lettuce.

Train the tomatoes as space-saving cordons (*see p.171*).

Deadhead your nasturtiums to keep them flowering well.

4 Harvest pea shoots just above the lowest leaves, when they are about 6in (15cm) tall. The plants will resprout to give another harvest in a few weeks.

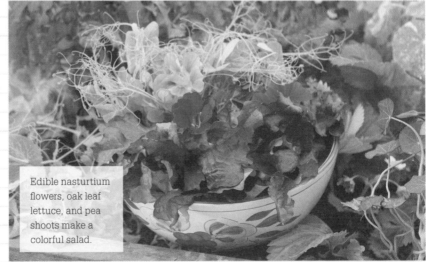

Edible nasturtium flowers, oak leaf lettuce, and pea shoots make a colorful salad.

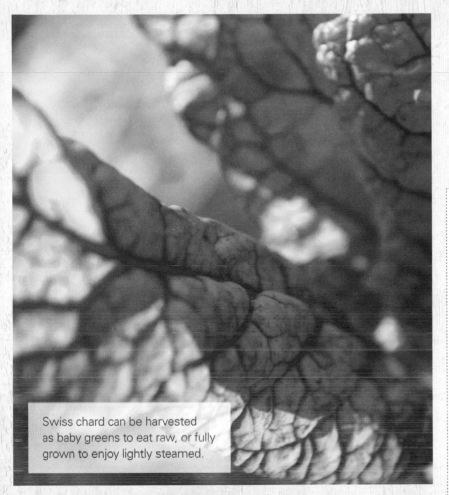

Swiss chard can be harvested as baby greens to eat raw, or fully grown to enjoy lightly steamed.

TRAIN TOMATOES

When there isn't a lot of room for bush varieties, cordon tomatoes are an excellent option. These are grown as a single stem that is trained up a vertical support, such as a pole or string. Any sideshoots that appear in the leaf joints should be pinched off (*left*), and the main growing tip is removed once the plant has produced 5–6 trusses of tomatoes. If you have more space, bush tomatoes simply require support rather than training.

Always wash your hands after handling tomato plants. The sap can irritate skin. Or, wear gloves.

Tomato tips

Choice toms Try growing unusual varieties of tomatoes, such as 'Green Zebra' (*above*), that you'd be hard pressed to find in shops.

Ripe fruit Small cherry tomatoes are the best type for cooler areas—they ripen more quickly than larger-fruiting types.

Fall

As summer crops finish, plant out hardy ones raised from seed in pots during summer, such as Swiss chard, to harvest until winter.

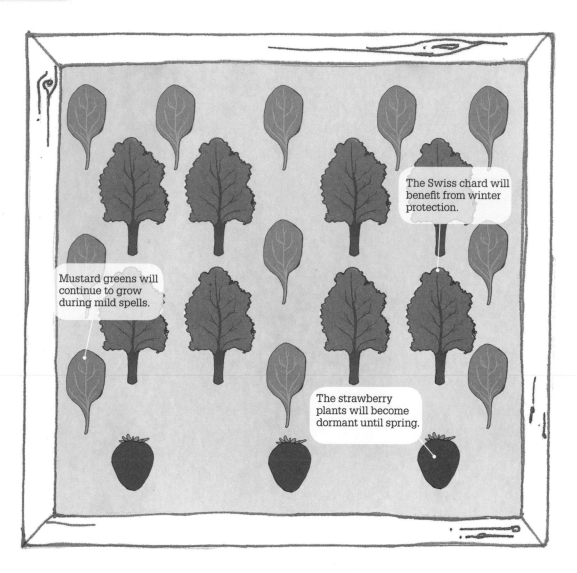

The soil in your raised bed will still be warm in fall, and although the temperatures are lower, it is still warm enough to grow certain crops. Take advantage of these favorable conditions for as long as they last, and grow and harvest as much as you can.

Alternative crops to grow

Spring

Carrots
Instead of peas Sow seeds thinly where they are to grow in spring. Pull in early summer.

Beets
Instead of peas Sow seeds into the soil in early spring. Pull the tender roots in early summer.

Radishes
Instead of green onions Sow the seeds directly, water well, and pull when large enough.

Violas
Instead of nasturtiums Plant out young plants in early spring. Pick the flowers into summer.

Summer

Marjoram
Instead of pea shoots Plant out in early summer. Pick the aromatic leaves all summer.

Spinach
Instead of lettuce Sow into the bed in mid-spring and harvest from summer to fall.

Basil
Instead of nasturtiums Plant young plants in summer and harvest regularly all season.

Sweet corn
Instead of tomatoes Plant out young plants in early summer in a block. Harvest in late summer.

Fall

Winter-flowering violas
Instead of mustard greens Plant in fall and harvest the flowers until spring.

Black leaf kale
Instead of Swiss chard Sow seed in pots in early summer to plant out in late summer.

Arugula
Instead of mustard greens Sow the seed into any free space and harvest once large enough.

DECIDING WHAT TO PLANT

No sowing plans are set in stone and it's important to grow what you love to eat. If you're not interested in growing green onions, lettuce, tomatoes, or peas, here are some alternatives to try.

Gourmet bed

When space is limited, think gourmet, and fill your bed with crop varieties that you could never find in the supermarket. They offer a superior taste and often look fantastic, but take no more time and effort to grow than ordinary crops.

Look out for **unusual** or **heirloom** varieties of **tomatoes**, **carrots**, and **beets** to enjoy their **subtly different tastes**, **colors**, and **textures**. Why grow the same **zucchini** that you can **easily buy**? Try **tromboncino** ones instead, with their **amazing fruit**, and grow them **alongside** lemony-tasting **purple oxalis** leaves.

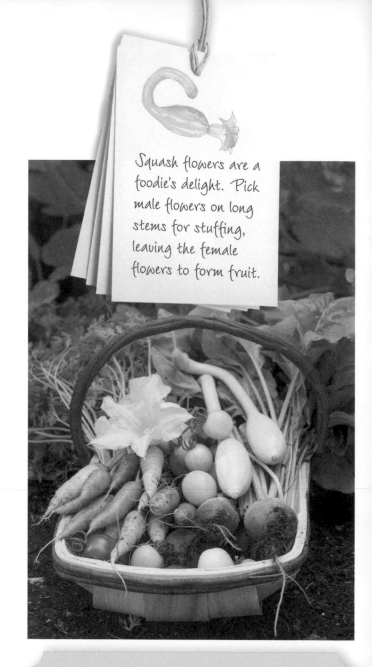

Squash flowers are a foodie's delight. Pick male flowers on long stems for stuffing, leaving the female flowers to form fruit.

You will need

■ **Materials**

Raised bed, approximately 3ft (1m) square
Multipurpose soil mix, topsoil, and grit
Liquid fertilizer

3 x bamboo poles, about 8ft (2.5m) tall
Garden string
Trellis
Cloche for spring protection

Spring to summer

Fall to spring

READY FOR SUMMER After the last frost, plant the tomato and tromboncino zucchini, and provide support. Also plant the oxalis. The other summer crops can be sown from seed.

INTO WINTER Keep your bed productive with frilly endives, sown in fall for winter harvest, and garlic and broad beans, which will be ready next spring and summer.

CROPS—WHEN TO SOW OR PLANT

Zucchini 'Tromboncino'
Plant mid- to late spring

Tomato 'Snowberry'
Plant mid-spring

Tomato 'Beam's Yellow Pear'
Plant mid-spring

Tomato 'Black Cherry'
Plant mid-spring

Marigolds
Sow early spring
Plant late spring

Carrot 'Harlequin'
Sow mid-spring

Beet 'Boltardy'
Sow mid- to late spring

Beet 'Burpees Golden'
Sow mid- to late spring

Purple oxalis
(*Oxalis triangularis*)
Plant late spring

Endive 'Wallone Despa'
Sow/plant late summer

Broad bean 'Super Aquadulche'
Sow late fall

Garlic
Plant late fall

Reclaimed steel mesh is ideal for zucchini to climb.

Fill with an even blend of soil mix and topsoil, and 10% grit.

Spring

Tomatoes and zucchini can be grown from seed in spring, or bought as young plants. After the last frost, harden them off and plant them out.

1 Tomatoes and summer squash are hungry plants, so add homemade compost or enriched multipurpose soil mix to the bed.

2 Make a hole for the zucchini wider and deeper than the pot. This vigorous plant will fill the space, so don't be tempted to plant two.

3 Plant with the neck of the plant just above the surface of the soil to avoid neck rot. Cover with soil mix, firm in well, and water it thoroughly.

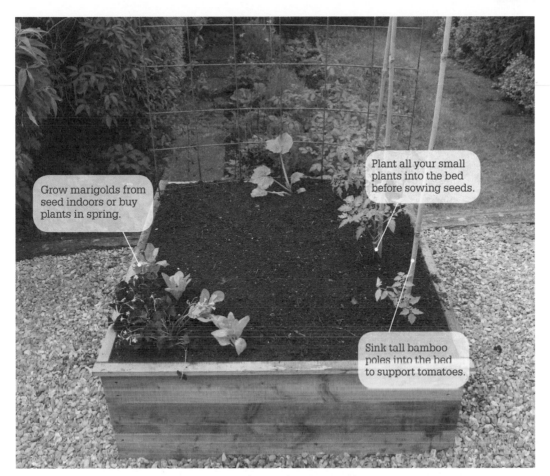

Grow marigolds from seed indoors or buy plants in spring.

Plant all your small plants into the bed before sowing seeds.

Sink tall bamboo poles into the bed to support tomatoes.

4 Plant your tomatoes next to their poles and tie in the stems with string. Water them well and continue to tie them in as they grow.

5 Harden off your marigolds and oxalis plants, and plant them out after the last frost. Snip off any dead leaves to encourage new growth.

6 Sow carrot and beet seeds in furrows, cover them lightly, and water gently. Check planting distances in the Crop planner (*see pp.224–241*).

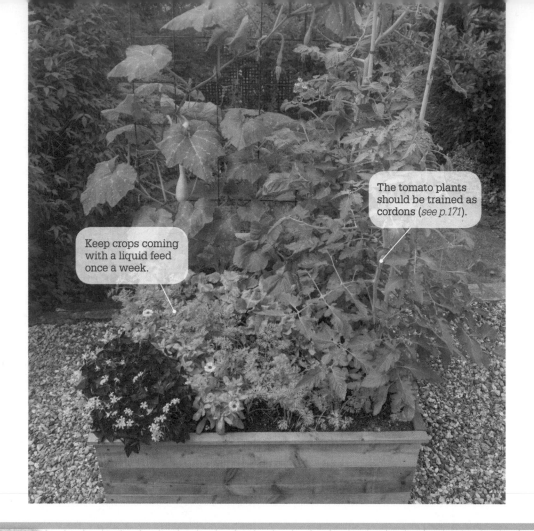

Keep crops coming with a liquid feed once a week.

The tomato plants should be trained as cordons (*see p.171*).

(*see p.171*)

Summer

By early summer your bed will be bursting with produce, rewarding your hard work. Harvest regularly, and keep your crops well watered and fed.

1 Your squash will cling on and climb rapidly, but watch out for growth heading off in a direction you hadn't planned on; redirect it and tie it in.

2 Thin out carrots and beets to allow decent-sized roots to form. Eat tiny carrots raw and add young beet leaves to salads.

3 Start feeding tomatoes weekly with a tomato fertilizer once the first flowers appear. Keep the plants moist at all times to avoid the fruit splitting.

5 Lightly harvest the leaves from oxalis to use sparingly in summer salads. The leaves pack a strong, lemony punch, which comes from oxalic acid (also present in sorrel and spinach). Enjoy eating it in moderation.

4 Tromboncinos are at their best when they are 12–16in (30–40cm) long. Keep picking for a nonstop supply. Try shaving them with a potato peeler to use like pasta.

WHY RED?

Tomatoes come in a huge variety of colors and shapes—from dark reds to pale yellows and greens, and in all shapes from plums to light bulbs. All are grown in the same way, so why not choose one that isn't simply round and red?

WEEDING OUT WEEDS

A benefit of planting closely in your bed is that it helps to suppress weeds. However, they can still appear, unseen at first, between your plants, and will compete for water and nutrients. Check regularly, and remove any you spot.

6 The mix of soil in a raised bed, and its lack of rocks, makes it ideal for growing carrots with perfectly formed roots. For a selection of colorful, crunchy, and sweet-tasting roots, grow 'Harlequin' (*right*). If you would prefer single colors, choose 'Cosmic Purple', 'Atomic Red', or 'Solar Yellow'.

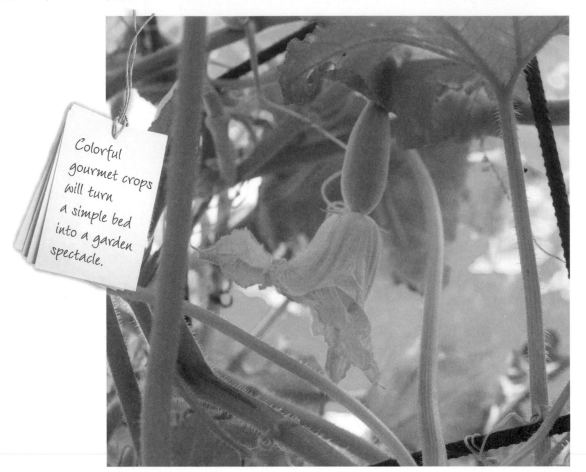

Colorful gourmet crops will turn a simple bed into a garden spectacle.

Summer

From mid- to late summer there should be something to eat every day: fresh beets and carrots and trusses of tomatoes, ripening in the sun.

1 Pull beets when the tops of the roots are visible above the soil surface. You can also eat the leaves young and raw or mature and cooked.

2 Pull carrots gently to avoid snapping the roots and disturbing the rest of the crop. Make this easier by watering the soil or loosening it slightly first.

3 To encourage a larger harvest, pick your tomatoes regularly. They are at their best when they are fully ripe, pull easily, and are slightly soft.

Fall to Spring

Clear the bed in fall and dig in fresh soil mix
for crops that will take you through to next summer.

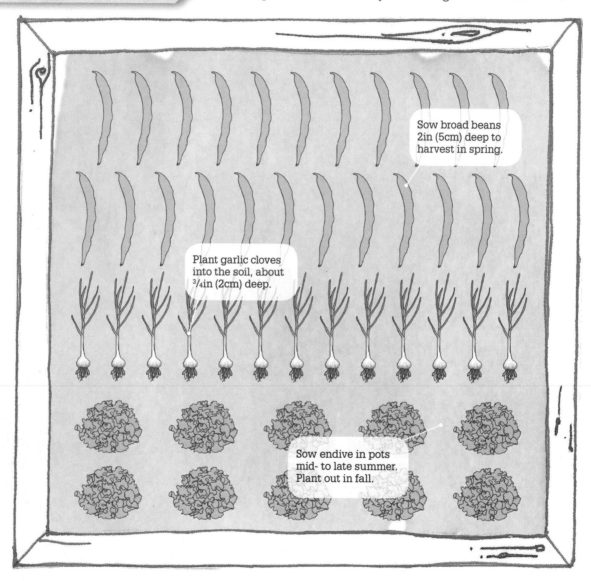

Sow broad beans
2in (5cm) deep to
harvest in spring.

Plant garlic cloves
into the soil, about
³/₄in (2cm) deep.

Sow endive in pots
mid- to late summer.
Plant out in fall.

Sow broad beans from mid-fall to crop in early spring. A late-fall
planting of garlic will be ready to harvest in summer, while endive
will keep you in flavorful leaves throughout the winter.
In colder spells, protect your plants with fabric or cloches.

Alternative crops to grow

Spring to Summer

Cornflowers
Instead of marigolds Use these attractive, edible flowers to add color to salads. Sow in spring.

Sweet peppers
Instead of tomatoes Peppers enjoy the same conditions as tomatoes. Plant in early summer.

Kohlrabi
Instead of carrots Sow this gourmet vegetable from mid-spring onward (see p.229).

Spinach
Instead of endive Sow seed in pots during summer to plant out in early fall (see p.230).

Green or runner beans
Instead of tromboncinos Use either crop to cover the vertical support. Sow in early summer.

Alpine strawberries
Instead of oxalis These can be planted as young plants during spring, and will fruit all summer.

Summer herbs
Instead of oxalis Plant thyme and marjoram in spring, and harvest throughout the summer.

Florence fennel
Instead of carrots Sow directly in early summer, keep moist, and harvest the stems in summer.

Winter to Spring

Chicory
Instead of endive Sow in pots in summer, ready to plant them out when the bed is cleared.

Black leaf kale
Instead of broad beans Sow in pots in summer. Insert poles for support and harvest all winter.

Swiss chard
Instead of endive Sow during late summer in pots, and plant them out in early fall.

Sprouting broccoli
Instead of broad beans Raise plants in pots from seed sown in summer. Harvest until spring.

Circular salad bed

A raised bed can be used to create dazzling decorative effects that are also productive. Try growing your own crop circles—rings of mixed salad leaves and edible flowers, with trailing tomatoes on the perimeter. Site the bed in a sunny spot on a patio, so you can go out and pick leaves as and when you need them.

In yards where **space** is **limited** there is **always** a **compromise** between **how much room** you devote to **flowers**, and how much you **allocate to crops**. The **virtue** of this **planting design**, with its **colorful** and **edible fruit**, **greens**, and **flowers**, is that it **tastes** as **good as it looks**.

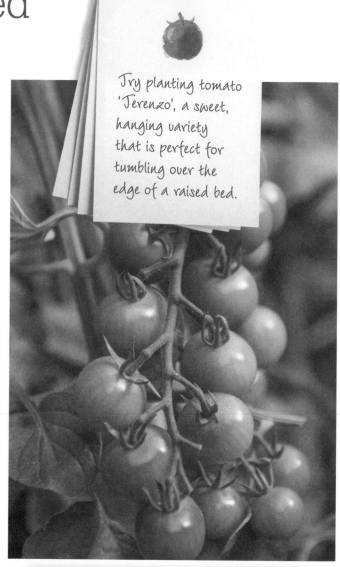

Try planting tomato 'Terenzo', a sweet, hanging variety that is perfect for tumbling over the edge of a raised bed.

You will need

▪ **Materials**

Raised bed, approximately 3ft (1m) square

Multipurpose soil mix, topsoil, and grit

Horticultural sand

Liquid fertilizer

Cloches and fabric for winter protection

Spring to Summer

Fall to Winter

FRESH SALADS are the main focus of the summer bed, sown and planted from mid- to late spring to provide a continuous supply of greens and sweet cherry tomatoes.

COLORFUL KALE and spicy mustard greens, sown in summer and planted in fall, maintain a handsome bed of salad crops and stir-fry vegetables through the winter.

CROPS—WHEN TO SOW OR PLANT

 Tomato 'Terenzo' Plant late spring

 Lettuce 'Navarra' Sow mid-spring

 Lettuce 'Lobjoits' Sow mid-spring

 Violas Plant mid-spring

 Chives Plant 1 mid-spring

 Garlic 'Solent White' Plant in fall

 Kale 'Redbor' and 'Winterbor' Sow midsummer

 Mustard greens 'Red frills' Sow in summer

 Mibuna Sow in summer

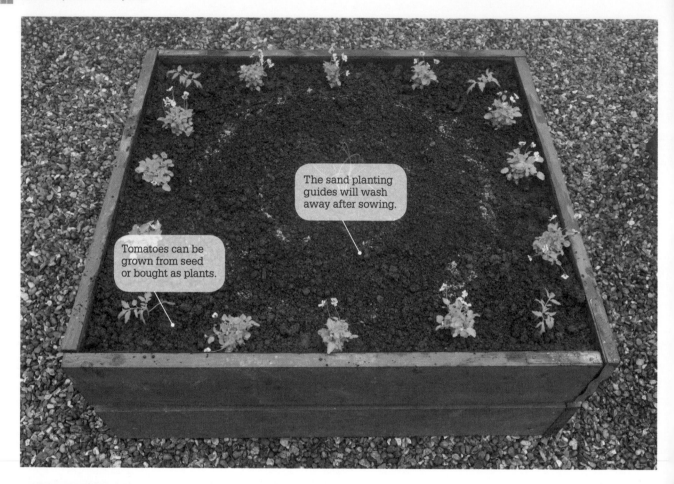

Summer

For summer crops, work begins in late spring, preparing your bed for sowing seeds directly into the soil, and for planting out plants after the last frost.

1 If using an existing bed, prepare the soil by turning it over, remove any weeds, and top it off. For a new bed, fill it with the ideal mix (*see p.23*).

2 Rake the soil to a fine tilth, ready for sowing. Attach string to a peg in the middle of the bed and tie a dibble to the other end. Mark out circles.

3 Check your seed packets for the ideal planting distances for your crops. Space the circles accordingly, and mark them out, using sand.

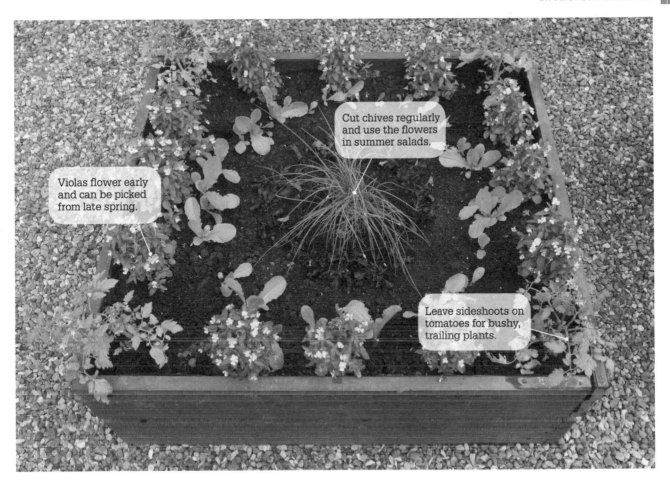

Cut chives regularly and use the flowers in summer salads.

Violas flower early and can be picked from late spring.

Leave sideshoots on tomatoes for bushy, trailing plants.

4 Put a chive plant in the center of the bed, with a trailing tomato plant in each corner to cascade over the edges. Firm and water the plants in.

5 Sow lettuce seeds thinly into the furrows, following the lines of the sand. Cover with soil and water in gently, using a watering can.

GENERAL CARE
DON'T FORGET TO:
- Keep to the circles as you sow, and remove seedlings that spoil the design
- Protect young plants from slugs, snails, and birds
- Keep watering, even in wet spells
- Weed between plants regularly
- Harvest young salad greens regularly
- Give tomatoes a liquid feed when the first flowers and trusses begin to form

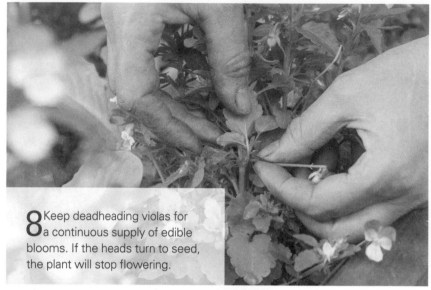

8 Keep deadheading violas for a continuous supply of edible blooms. If the heads turn to seed, the plant will stop flowering.

6 Space the viola plants evenly around the edge of the bed in a wide circle. Tuck them into holes, firm them in, and water them thoroughly.

9 Cut the chives as and when you need them. For a fresh new crop, cut the leaves clear down in midsummer—they will quickly grow back. Chives will overwinter, and can be divided up in spring and replanted in fresh soil mix in a sunny location.

7 As lettuce begins to grow, thin it out so that the remaining plants can mature fully. Use the thinnings as an early crop, adding the succulent, sweet greens to salads.

LETTUCE GROW

Rather than pulling up the whole head of your lettuce plants at one time, you can leave the plant in place and harvest the outer leaves as you need them. Alternatively, cut the head off near the base, leaving a short stump that will regrow. Good varieties to plant include speckle-leaf 'Freckles' and bronze-tipped 'Rubens Red'.

Winter

As crops begin to fade at the end of the summer, clear the bed of debris and top it off with soil mix, ready to plant crops for winter and next summer.

Pick the outer leaves of kale, leaving inner ones to mature.

Plant garlic cloves ¾in (2cm) deep in fall.

Mustard greens are welcome in winter when salad is scarce.

For crops to grow through winter, sow kale and mustard greens in small pots during summer and let them grow, ready to plant out once your summer crops have been cleared. Garlic can be planted directly in the fall. Protect your salad greens with fabric or cloches during winter.

Alternative crops to grow

Summer

African basil
Instead of chives Plant out a pot-grown specimen once the risk of frost has passed. Harvest the leaves and stems during summer.

Cilantro
Instead of chives Sow seeds directly in early summer and keep the plants moist. Enjoy the flavorful leaves all summer.

Strawberries
Instead of tomatoes Plant strawberries in spring, and choose summer-fruiting and everbearing varieties for the longest harvest.

Spinach
Instead of summer lettuce Sow the seeds directly in late spring and keep the plants well watered. Harvest summer to winter.

Hyssop
Instead of violas Plant out small plants during spring and harvest the richly aromatic leaves and flowers throughout the summer.

Winter

Swiss chard
Instead of kale Sow the seeds into small pots in summer, let them grow, and plant out in fall. Harvest the leaves in winter.

Sprouting broccoli
Instead of kale Sow the seeds in pots in summer to grow. Plant in fall, staking them, and harvest in winter and spring.

Endive
Instead of mustard greens Sow the seeds during summer into small pots outside. Plant them out once the bed has been cleared.

Use your beds to grow the crops...
You love!

One of the **pleasures** of **growing your own** is that you can **concentrate** on **the crops** that you really **enjoy eating**. Lettuce may be **easy to grow**, but if you don't like it, **why bother**? Growing your own also means you can experiment with **different varieties** that you **never see** in the stores. If you love summer salads, **explore every possibility**, from textural Asian greens to peppery mustard greens. **If you like it, grow it**.

The Med bed

This bed brims with an essence of the Mediterranean, with its vibrant colors and flavors. Best in a warm spot, site your raised bed in the sunniest and most protected corner. Hold back from planting and sowing until the sun is high and the soil has warmed up in late spring.

Tap into the **tastes** and **health benefits** of a **Mediterranean diet** by growing **vibrant chili** and **sweet peppers**, crunchy **Florence fennel**, and **glossy eggplant**. Look for varieties that have been **selected** to **grow outdoors** in slightly cooler climates, and **pamper your plants** during prolonged **wet and cool** spells.

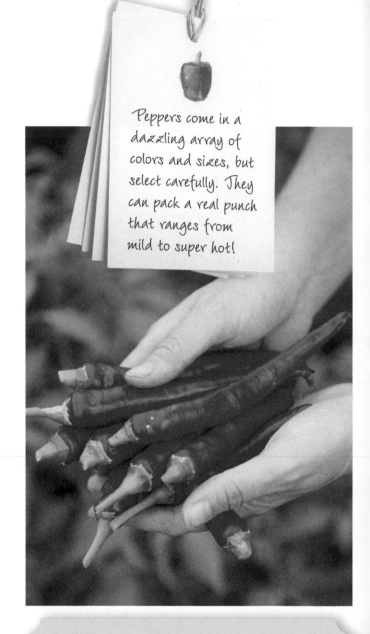

Peppers come in a dazzling array of colors and sizes, but select carefully. They can pack a real punch that ranges from mild to super hot!

You will need

- **Materials**

Raised bed approximately 3ft (1m) square	Bamboo poles
Topsoil, soil mix, and grit	Soft string
Watering can	Fabric or cloches for protection
Liquid ferilizer	

Summer

Winter

START THE SUMMER BED in late spring with chili peppers, bought as small plants, and Florence fennel, sweet peppers, and eggplant grown from seed indoors and planted out.

FOR WINTER CROPS clear the bed in early fall and sow radicchio and winter lettuce. Plant out kale, chicory, and sprouting broccoli, grown in pots during summer.

CROPS—WHEN TO SOW OR PLANT

Sweet Pepper
Sow indoors in pots early spring

Florence fennel
Sow indoors in pots early spring

Chicory
Sow in pots in midsummer

Lettuce 'Merveille de Quatre Saisons'
Sow seed directly in fall

Chili Pepper
Plant out in late spring

Sweet Pepper
Sow indoors in pots early spring

Kale
Sow in pots in midsummer

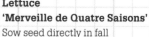
Sprouting broccoli
Sow in pots in midsummer

Chili Pepper
Plant out in late spring

Eggplant
Sow indoors in pots early spring

Radicchio 'Orchidea Rossa'
Sow in fall

DON'T DISTURB

Eggplant dislikes root disturbance. Plant seeds singly in pots indoors in spring, and ensure the plants have a good root system before you plant them outside. Acclimatize the plants to life outdoors by hardening them off over a couple of weeks. Plant out gently in warm soil in full sun, and insert a pole for support.

Cooler summer This bed is definitely one for warmer areas—in cooler spots or during a cold, wet summer you may struggle to produce a ripe eggplant or more than a handful of sweet peppers. It's worth trying, and if any plants wilt or fail, replace them with Mediterranean herbs, such as rosemary and basil, and sow fast-growing salad greens.

TOO CHILLY FOR CHILI PEPPERS?

Both chili and sweet peppers are tender plants and suffer in cold, wet soil. Harden them off well before planting, and make sure that the soil in your bed has warmed up. Putting a cloche over the planting area for a week or two will help to create a welcoming spot.

Summer

In early summer, Florence fennel can be sown from seed under cover, to plant out in a few weeks' time. Later harvests can be sown directly.

1 Sow three fennel seeds per pot under cover in late spring and thin to one healthy seedling, or sow directly outdoors in early summer.

2 Plant out with minimal disturbance after the last frost. Fennel plants tend to bolt if they are disturbed, or are too cold or underwatered.

SOME LIKE IT HOT AND DRY

Peppers hate to be wet, so water this crop minimally and let the top of the soil dry out between waterings. Most chili peppers ripen from green to red, becoming spicier as they do so. As long as the fruit have reached their full size, you can pick them when they are green for a milder flavor. Picking unripe fruit will also encourage the plant to keep flowering and produce more.

When your eggplant is about 10in (25cm) tall, pinch off the top of the main shoot to encourage bushier growth. Once the plant starts flowering, feed it weekly with liquid tomato fertilizer to promote fruiting.

Some sweet peppers grow tall and may need supporting with a bamboo pole. Feed plants regularly with tomato fertilizer once in flower, and harvest the mature fruit to encourage more.

FUSS OVER FENNEL

Fennel likes to be pampered, so keep your plants well watered, and mulch around the base of bulb to retain moisture. Pick some leaves to use in salads or to flavor food, leaving plenty to support the plants' growth. Harvest by pulling the bulbs out of the soil with the roots attached, or cut through the base of each bulb just below ground level. The remaining roots should then produce another small flush of airy, anise-flavored leaves.

Winter As soon as the last peppers have been picked, fill the bed with kale, broccoli, chicory, and lettuce for a feast from fall to spring.

Underplant kale and sprouting broccoli with chicory.

Black leaf kale will be a statuesque presence in the bed.

Plant radicchio where it is easy to harvest.

In early fall clear the bed and dig in fresh potting mix. With planning, your winter crops will be underway, sown and growing in pots from midsummer. In fall, some winter salads can be sown directly. Protect plants with fabric or cloches in cold spells.

Alternative crops to grow

Summer

Runner beans
Instead of peppers Sow beans directly in late spring and train the plants up tepees.

Tomatoes
Instead of eggplant Plant cordon tomatoes in late spring. Tie them in to bamboo poles.

Summer squash
Instead of peppers Train the plants up trellises or tepees to make the best use of space.

Sweet corn
Instead of eggplant Sow seeds in early summer or plant out small plants raised in pots.

Cucamelons
Instead of fennel These delicate vines will scramble up a tepee or trellis. Sow in spring.

Basil
Instead of peppers Sow inside, plant out mid-spring, and pinch off tops for bushy growth.

Dwarf green beans
Instead of peppers No supports needed for these productive plants about 18in (45cm) high.

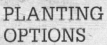

PLANTING OPTIONS

If eggplant and fennel are not to your taste, there's a range of crops shown here that will thrive in similar warm, sunny conditions through summer, or which will fill the bed in winter. See the Crop planner on pages 224–241 for more alternatives to grow.

Winter

Swiss chard
Instead of kale Start off Swiss chard in small pots in summer for colorful stems and tasty leaves.

Corn salad
Instead of radicchio Sow seed during summer in seed flats and transplant in early fall.

Mustard greens
Instead of lettuce Interplant broccoli with spicy green and red varieties. Sow in summer.

Red Russian kale
Instead of broccoli Sow red and purple kale in pots in summer for a vibrant winter bed.

Shady bed

Not every gardener can rely on full sun throughout the day, especially on urban sites surrounded by houses and fences. This bed embraces shady spots, with plantings of vegetables, such as lettuce, sorrel, and mustard greens, that thrive in cool growing conditions.

Try for a **decorative effect** in your **cool corner** by planting quadrants of **shade-tolerant** crops that are **gloriously tasty**, too. Red-flecked **Lettuce 'Speckles'** and red-leaved **'Navarra'** are **stars** of the summer bed. **In fall, Mizuna** 'Red Knight', **Mustard green** 'Green in Snow', and **bok choy** continue the show.

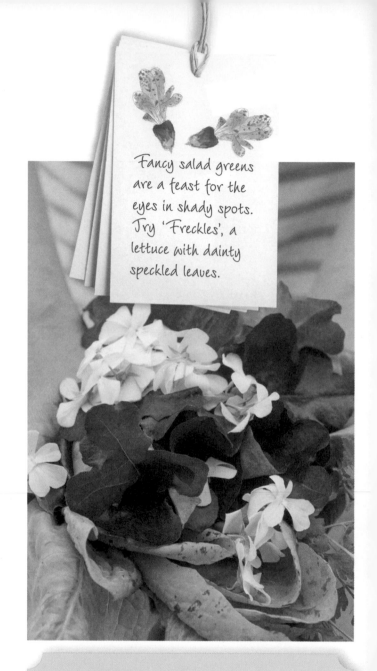

Fancy salad greens are a feast for the eyes in shady spots. Try 'Freckles', a lettuce with dainty speckled leaves.

You will need

- **Materials**
A raised bed approximately 3ft (1m) square
Topsoil, soil mix, and grit
Garden string
Short bamboo stakes

Watering can
Fabric and cloches for winter protection

Spring

GETTING STARTED After the final frost, plant small parsley plants, violas, and a sorrel centerpiece. Sow radishes and lettuce varieties to harvest in early summer.

Summer

REPLENISH While the soil is still warm in late summer, clear the bed and resow it with fall and winter crops, such as mustard greens, bok choy, and chicory.

CROPS—WHEN TO SOW OR PLANT

Sorrel
Plant small plants or sow seeds in mid-spring

Violas
Plant small plants or sow seeds in mid-spring

Parsley
Plant or sow in mid-spring

Radishes
Sow at intervals from spring to late summer

Lettuce
Sow regularly from spring until midsummer

Bok choy
Sow seeds direct in late summer

Mizuna
Sow mid- to late summer

Mustard greens
Sow seeds direct in late summer

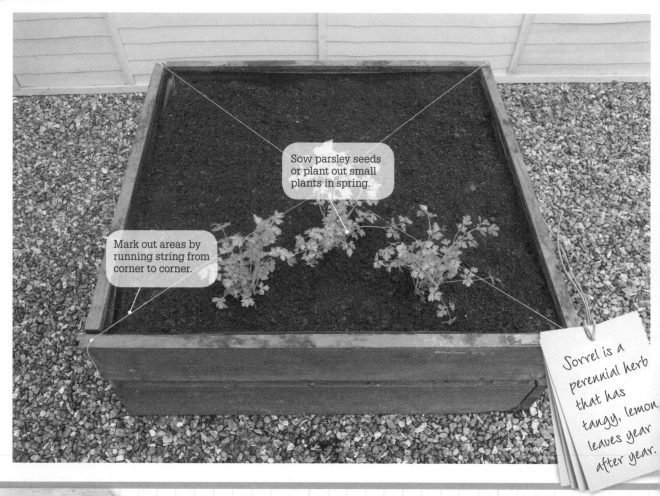

Sow parsley seeds or plant out small plants in spring.

Mark out areas by running string from corner to corner.

Sorrel is a perennial herb that has tangy, lemon leaves year after year.

Spring

Mark out your plot and plant potted herbs before sowing seeds. Your seedlings should start appearing within a week, and radishes may be ready in 3-4 weeks.

1 Sow seeds in clearly defined rows. This makes it easy to identify weeds and pick them so that there is no competition for nutrients and water.

2 When the seedlings are bigger and have developed true leaves, thin them out carefully, leaving the remainder at their final spacings.

3 Radishes grow rapidly. As soon as seedlings appear, thin them out to 2in (5cm) apart to allow space for roots to develop quickly.

Sow more radishes every two weeks for a nonstop harvest.

Thin out the lettuce to their preferred planting distance.

Cut the parsley tops to prevent it from going to seed.

4 Don't throw away your thinnings. These young tender leaves, along with young radish and sorrel leaves, make a delicious, herby salad.

5 Brighten up your salads with sweet-scented viola flowers in all shades from violet to pale yellow. Pick them regularly to keep the plants flowering.

6 Harvest radishes young, as soon as their crowns show above the soil. Left to grow too big, the roots become tough and will lose their crispness.

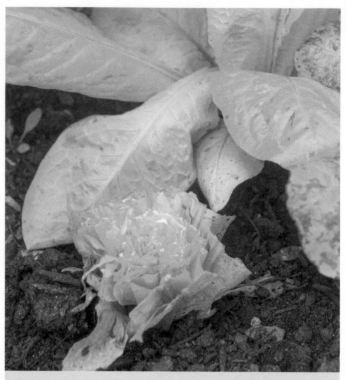

HARVEST LETTUCE by picking off the outer leaves and leaving the heads to grow, or by cutting the fully grown, hearty head off at the base. If you leave the stump in the soil, it will regrow, with leaves to harvest again in summer.

Spring

Keep up a nonstop supply of salad crops by resowing whenever space becomes free.

1 Radishes take little room and grow fast in the summer heat, so after each harvest, level and rake over the soil, and sow a fresh row.

2 Resow lettuces too, keeping them well watered to prevent them from bolting and going to seed.

Shady areas are havens for slugs and snails. Go on patrol after rain or at dusk and deal with them.

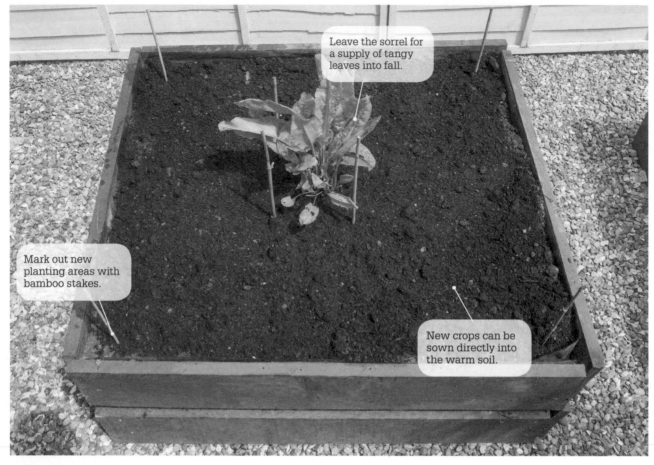

Leave the sorrel for a supply of tangy leaves into fall.

Mark out new planting areas with bamboo stakes.

New crops can be sown directly into the warm soil.

Summer

As soon as the last lettuce and radishes have been harvested, seize the opportunity to sow more leafy vegetables that will take you through fall.

1 Dig some fresh soil mix into the bed and rake it to a fine tilth before sowing sugar loaf chicory, mustard greens, and bok choy.

2 When the seedlings have developed their first true leaves, thin them to 6–12in (15–30cm) apart. Use the thinned seedlings for salads.

3 Bok choy leaves will be ready in about a month; fully grown heads for stir-frying take up to two months. Water well to prevent bolting.

Alternative crops to grow

Summer

Sweet cicely
Instead of Sorrel Plant this delicious aniseed-flavored herb as a small plant in spring.

Tatsoi
Instead of lettuce Directly sow this gorgeous Asian green, a rosette bok choy, in early spring.

Spinach
Instead of lettuce Sow spinach from spring onward. Use young greens in salads.

Oriental saladini
Instead of lettuce Grow a mix of mustard greens and Asian greens to cut-and-come-again.

Lettuce 'Maravilla de Verano Canasta'
Instead of 'Freckles' Try this red- and green-leaf variety.

Swiss chard
Instead of lettuce Sow in spring to supply young leaves and brilliantly colored stems.

Chervil
Instead of parsley This ferny herb has an aniseed flavor. Sow in spring and summer.

COOL CUSTOMERS

For your shady bed, seek out varieties that have been selected for their resilience in cool climates, especially for your fall crops. A cool corner in summer can become a frost pocket in winter. Use fabric and cloches to protect delicate leaves.

Fall

Corn salad
Instead of chicory Sow seeds directly in late summer for crops throughout the winter.

Arugula
Instead of mustard greens Sow seed directly from mid- to late summer and pick regularly.

Miner's lettuce
Instead of chicory Eat both the greens and flowers of this crop, sown directly in summer.

Kale
Instead of bok choy Grow one of the many varieties of kale, sown directly in midsummer.

Liven up your cooking with...
Fresh herbs!

Instead of growing **fruit and vegetables**, you could devote a raised bed to **culinary herbs**. Choose your favorite **annual and perennial** types, such as **basil** and **chives**, and also include **evergreens**, like sage, that you can **pick through the winter**. Many **common herbs** can be **bought fresh** in supermarkets, so why not plant others that aren't, such as **aromatic sweet cicely**?

Tasty herb bed

This decorative, deliciously scented, and intensely flavored group of plants is tailor-made for a small bed. Keep them close by for easy picking. This is a valuable crop for any cook who likes to experiment—cut herbs in stores are pricey, limited in scope, and bear no comparison to homegrown.

Many of these herbs are **perennials**, returning **year after year**, which makes this bed **easy to maintain**. Plant staples, like **sage and thyme**, and unusual herbs, such as **lovage**, **fennel**, **and sweet cicely**, which you are **unlikely** to ever find **in the grocery store**. **Edible flowers**, such as starflowers, **self-seed freely**, providing **free plants** next year.

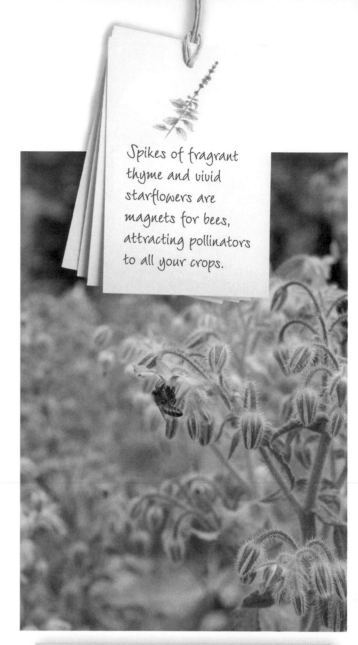

Spikes of fragrant thyme and vivid starflowers are magnets for bees, attracting pollinators to all your crops.

You will need

▪ Materials

Raised bed approximately 3ft (1m) square

Topsoil, soil mix, and grit.

Stakes for tall plants

Tools

Watering can

Trowel

Summer

PLANTING TIME Plant small herb plants in mid-spring as the soil warms up. Wait until after the last frost to plant basil and fennel. Sow California poppies around the herbs.

Winter

WINTER HERBS Replace starflowers, cilantro, and poppies when they go to seed, with mustard greens and arugula. Leave the perennials, and plant garlic in late fall.

HERBS—WHEN TO SOW AND PLANT

Rosemary
Perennial, plant mid-spring

Lovage
Tall perennial, plant mid-spring

Sweet cicely
Perennial, plant mid-spring

Marjoram
Perennial, plant mid-spring

Mustard greens
Annual, sow in late summer

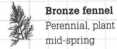
Bronze fennel
Perennial, plant mid-spring

Starflower
Annual, sow late spring

Purple sage
Evergreen shrub, plant mid-spring

California poppy
Annual, sow in late spring

Arugula
Annual, sow in late summer

Thyme
Perennial, plant mid-spring

Cilantro
Annual, sow or plant late spring

Purple basil
Annual, plant late spring

Garlic
Plant cloves in fall

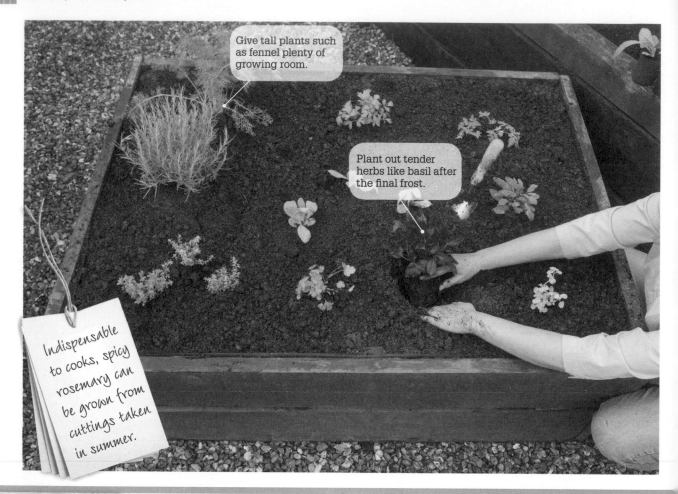

Give tall plants such as fennel plenty of growing room.

Plant out tender herbs like basil after the final frost.

Indispensable to cooks, spicy rosemary can be grown from cuttings taken in summer.

Summer

Purchase a mix of small hardy and annual herb plants from a good herb nursery to plant in mid-spring, spaced evenly around the bed.

1 Mediterranean plants such as thyme, rosemary, sage, and fennel need full sun to grow their best. Ease them gently from their pots.

2 This group of herbs is sensitive to wet soil, and should not be planted any deeper than they were in their original containers.

3 To help pot-grown plants establish well, use your fingers to gently loosen their root balls. This encourages new roots to grow into the soil.

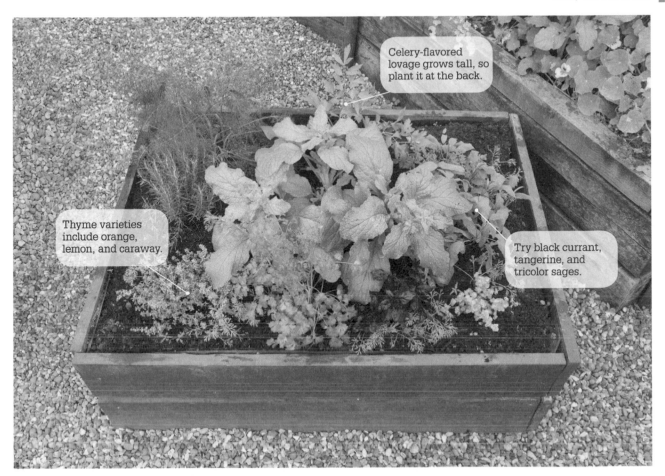

Celery-flavored lovage grows tall, so plant it at the back.

Thyme varieties include orange, lemon, and caraway.

Try black currant, tangerine, and tricolor sages.

4 Purple basil is slower-growing than the green-leaf type. Make sure it isn't smothered by neighboring plants as they grow. Trim back if necessary.

5 Leave fennel to develop beautiful flower heads in late summer. These are loved by bees, and will supply aniseed-flavored seeds for cooking.

GENERAL CARE
DON'T FORGET TO:
- Keep all your plants well watered
- Check for slugs and snails regularly
- Keep trimming your herbs to prevent them from flowering early
- Remove dead or fading leaves
- Pick herb bunches in late summer and dry for winter, or freeze them
- Cover tender shoots, like basil, with a net if birds start feasting on them

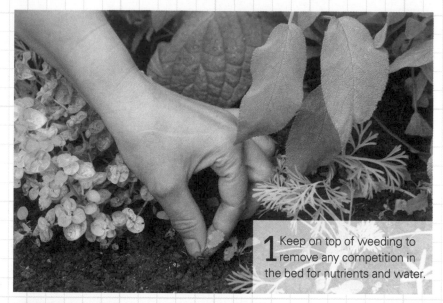

1 Keep on top of weeding to remove any competition in the bed for nutrients and water.

2 Young starflower leaves bring a mild cucumber flavor to salads, and the flowers can be picked off and frozen into ice cubes to decorate fruity drinks. If you have too many starflowers, dig young plants back into the soil as a green manure.

MAKE THE MOST OF MARJORAM

Marjoram 'Golden Curly' is a decorative, perennial herb. It produces prolific tufts of bright leaves and frothy pale pink flowers that hum with bees in summer. Marjoram is in the same family as oregano and adds rich flavor to pasta sauces, pizzas, casseroles, and roasted vegetables.

Sowing annual herbs

Sow seed under cover during early summer into flats of multipurpose soil mix. Keep the seeds warm and moist.

Transplant the seedlings into individual pots once they are large enough to handle. Keep growing them under cover.

Pinch off the tips to encourage the plants to bush out. Harden them off for a few days, then plant them outside.

Winter

Fennel, hyssop, and sweet cicely die down in fall and shoot up again in spring, while rosemary and sage can be picked all winter.

When starflower is over, remove and sow rows of arugula.

To overwinter, thyme may need protection from frost.

Plant the garlic as individual cloves in early fall.

At the end of summer, gaps left in the bed by annuals can be sown with mustard green and arugula seeds for fall pickings. In late fall, plant garlic cloves, which can be picked as green leafy spikes in spring, and as succulent bulbs in summer.

Alternative herbs to grow

Summer

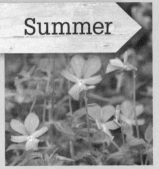

Violas
Instead of California poppies
Plant violas in spring and
crystallize the flowers for cakes.

Tree spinach
Instead of lovage This fast-
growing, 6ft (1.8m) annual has
magenta-colored young leaves.

Dill
Instead of fennel Sow in spring
for aniseed-flavored, feathery
leaves and seeds.

Mint
Instead of sweet cicely Keep
mint confined to its pot in the
bed to keep it from taking over.

Angelica
Instead of lovage This whopper
produces sweet stems to cook
with fruit and vegetables.

Salad burnet
Instead of marjoram Sow this
pretty perennial herb with a mild
cucumber flavor in mid-spring.

Hyssop
Instead of rosemary Plant in
early summer. It has aromatic
leaves and blue flower spikes.

Parsley
Instead of cilantro Sow this
versatile biennial in late spring.
Use in sauces and salads.

Winter

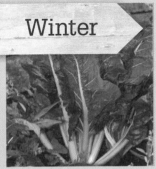

Swiss chard
Instead of arugula Harvest the
robust stems and crisp leaves in
winter. Sow in late summer.

Kale
Instead of mustard greens
Kales have wonderful textures
and colors. Sow in late summer.

Tatsoi
Instead of garlic Plant mid-
to late summer for succulent
greens in fall and winter.

PICK YOUR FAVORITES
Choose your own. There
are so many delicious
herbs, each with their own
flavor and special culinary
uses, but the most useful
to you are the ones you
include regularly in your
own dishes. Most are easy
to grow and many come
back year after year.

PLANT KNOW-HOW

Crop planner

Use this crop planner to help make the most of the space you have, and to decide what to sow and plant when. With careful planning, you'll be able to make use of every inch of your growing space, with new crops ready to plant as existing ones are reaching maturity.

A guide to the icons

 PLANT IN SUN OR PART SHADE These plants prefer either sun or part shade. Fruit and vegetables will not grow in full shade.

 TIME FROM SOWING TO HARVESTING This is a guide to how long each crop takes to reach maturity. Use it to plan the order in which you sow your crops.

 WHEN TO SOW SEED UNDER COVER This is when to sow seed in flats and pots. Keep the seedlings indoors until planted out.

 WHEN TO SOW SEED OUTSIDE Now is the time when you can sow each crop directly outside in the soil.

 WHEN TO PLANT OUT SEEDLINGS If you have raised plants from seed, or bought them as seedlings, this is when to plant them out.

 WHEN TO HARVEST This is the time of year when each crop should be ready to harvest.

 IDEAL DISTANCE BETWEEN PLANTS This is the distance to leave between your plants.

 SMALL SPACE RATING This is a guide to how productive a crop is, relative to the time and space they need. The crops awarded three stars are the most productive choices.

SWEET PEPPERS

- ☀ Full sun
- ⧗ 20–26 weeks
- ⌂ Late winter to mid-spring
- 🌱 Late spring to early summer
- 🌱 Early to midsummer
- 🧺 Midsummer to early fall
- ↔ 18–24in (45–60cm)
- ★★ Small space rating

Varieties to try
'Corno di Toro Rosso' Long, tapering scarlet peppers.
'Gourmet' Early-ripening, chunky orange fruit.
'Gypsy' Heavy-cropping, slim green peppers ripen to red.
How to grow Once planted out, support plants with poles because the fruit are heavy. Feed weekly with tomato fertilizer once the first flowers appear. You get more peppers if you pick them green, but fewer, sweeter fruit if you let them ripen and change color.

CHILI PEPPERS

- ☀ Full sun
- ⧗ 20–26 weeks
- ⌂ Late winter to mid-spring
- 🌱 Late spring to early summer
- 🌱 Late spring to early summer
- 🧺 Midsummer to early fall
- ↔ 18–24in (45–61cm)
- ★★★ Small space rating

Varieties to try
'Apache' Dwarf habit and small red fruit (medium-hot).
'Hungarian Hot Wax' Ripening to red and good for cool areas (mild).
'Prairie Fire' Masses of tiny yellow to red fruit all summer (hot).
How to grow Treat in a similar way to sweet peppers (above). Dwarf varieties also thrive on sunny windowsills in pots as small as 6in (15cm) across. Harvest over several weeks, green and mild, or hot and ripe. The fruit grow fewer but hotter if kept on the dry side.

TOMATOES

- ☀ Full sun
- ⧗ 9–12 weeks
- ⌂ Early spring
- 🌱 Mid- to late spring
- 🌾 Midsummer to fall
- ✋ Midsummer to early fall
- ↔ 12–36in (30–90cm)
- ★★★ Small space rating

Varieties to try
'Sungold' Sweet-tasting orange cherry-sized fruit.
'Gardener's Delight' Very reliable red cherry tomatoes.
'Green Zebra' Bears colorful yellow and green fruit.
How to grow Plant out deeper than in original pots, just below the first leaves. To grow cordon types, provide a tall support, and pinch off any sideshoots that develop, leaving a single stem. Once it has produced 5–6 trusses of fruit, pinch off the main tip. When growing bush varieties, the sideshoots are allowed to grow, and each will need a support. Keep all plants very well watered to prevent the fruit from splitting and, once in flower, feed weekly with tomato fertilizer.

EGGPLANT

- ☀ Full sun
- ⧗ 24–28 weeks
- ⌂ Early spring to mid-spring
- 🌱 Late spring to early summer
- 🌾 Late spring
- ✋ Late summer to mid-fall
- ↔ 24–30in (60–75cm)
- ★ Small space rating

Varieties to try
'Bonica' An early variety with purple-black fruit.
'Moneymaker' Tasty, purple fruit; grows well outdoors.
'Thai Green Pea' Abundant, slender, lime-green fruit.
How to grow Plants need rich, well-drained soil, warmth, and humidity, so are usually grown under cover in cool areas, or outside in sheltered, sunny spots. They dislike root disturbance, so sow seed singly in pots, planting them into containers or grow bags when the first flowers appear. Outdoor plants must be hardened off. Provide support and pinch off the growing tips to encourage bushiness. Water and feed well, and nip off the main tip once each plant has 4–6 fruits.

ZUCCHINI

- ☀ Full sun
- ⧗ 8–12 weeks
- ⌂ Late spring
- 🌱 Early summer
- 🌾 Early summer
- ✋ Midsummer to mid-fall
- ↔ 36in (90cm)
- ★★ Small space rating

Varieties to try
'Goldy' Prolific crops of bright yellow zucchini.
'Zucchini' Green fruit and an early cropper.
'Rond di Nice' Pale green round fruit, good for stuffing.
How to grow Harden off young plants before planting out in late spring, after the last frost, protecting them against slugs and snails. These are big plants, so position 3ft (90cm) apart, although they can also be grown in large containers. Keep plants very well watered, watering them directly at the base, and feed them regularly with a liquid tomato fertilizer once in fruit. Harvest zucchini when they reach 5–6in (13–15cm) long, taking care not to damage the main stem.

SUMMER SQUASH

- ☀ Full sun
- ⧗ 14–20 weeks
- ⌂ Mid-spring to late spring
- 🌱 Late spring to early summer
- 🌾 Early summer
- ✋ Midsummer to mid-fall
- ↔ 36in (90cm)
- ★★ Small space rating

Varieties to try
'Eight ball' Round, deep green, glossy squashes with nutty flesh.
'Peter Pan' Creamy flesh in pale green; a round, early squash.
'Sunburst' Yellow patty pan type squash with white flesh.
How to grow These fast-growing, large plants can be planted in the soil, or in containers or growing bags. Sow the large seed into pots, planting them out once the danger of frost has passed, or sow them directly outside. These plants are hungry and thirsty, but prone to rot, so keep the leaves and stems dry when watering the soil. Apply mulch and feed weekly with tomato fertilizer. Train the stems vertically to save space and to keep the fruit off the soil, where they may rot.

CUCUMBERS

- ☀ Full sun
- ⧗ 16–20 weeks
- ⌂ Early spring to mid-spring
- ⬟ Late spring to early summer
- �🌱 Early summer
- ⬤ Midsummer to mid-fall
- ↔ 18–36in (45–90cm)
- ★★★ Small space rating

Varieties to try
'Burpees Tasty Green' This bears long, tasty, crisp fruit.
'Crystal Apple' Outdoor type with small, round, sweet-tasting fruit.
'Marketmore' Outdoor ridge type with classic long, crisp fruit.
How to grow Cucumbers come in greenhouse or outdoor varieties; outdoor ones include short, rough-skinned ridge types. All need warmth, ample watering, rich soil, and a long season, so are sown indoors. Train the stems up poles to save space, and pinch off the tips when they reach the top. Keep plants well watered and feed regularly with tomato fertilizer. When growing greenhouse types, remove the male flowers (no fruitlet on stalk) to avoid bitter fruit.

CUCAMELONS

- ☀ Full sun
- ⧗ 12–16 weeks
- ⌂ Mid- to late spring
- ⬟ n/a
- 🌱 Late spring to early summer
- ⬤ Midsummer to early fall
- ↔ 12–16in (30–40cm)
- ★ Small space rating

Varieties to try
None available—Only the species is grown.
How to grow Although exotic-sounding, cucamelons are easy to grow, and can be treated in the same way as you would an outdoor cucumber. Sow indoors in late spring and plant out after the last frost into borders or large containers. The fruit are produced on long, thin, delicate vines that can be trained up tall supports, through other climbers, or allowed to trail. Keep plants well watered, and feed them using liquid tomato fertilizer to encourage a larger harvest. The green fruit, which have a sharp cucumber flavor, are ready to harvest when they reach the size of a chicken egg, and can be added to salads.

PEA SHOOTS

- ☀ Full sun or light shade
- ⧗ 1–2 weeks
- ⌂ All year
- ⬟ All year
- 🌱 Not applicable
- ⬤ All year
- ↔ 1in (2cm)
- ★★★ Small space rating

Varieties to try
'Oregon Sugar Pod' A hardy, disease-resistant snow pea type.
'Cascadia' A compact sugar snap pea that does not require support.
'Sugar Bon' A sugar snap pea, usually grown for its pods.
How to grow Sow any variety in succession every few weeks for a supply of tender shoots, leaves, and tendrils. Indoors, sow anytime in containers or growing bags, 1½in (4cm) deep, and 2–3in (5–8cm) apart. Sow outdoors in containers or open ground from early spring to early fall, or hardy varieties in mid- to late fall for early spring shoots. Keep seedlings moist and harvest when 4–6in (10–15cm) tall, pinching off the top 2–3in (5–8cm). You can re-harvest 3–4 times.

PEAS

- ☀ Full sun or part shade
- ⧗ 12–14 weeks
- ⌂ Spring or mid- to late fall
- ⬟ Spring
- 🌱 Mid-spring or late fall
- ⬤ Early summer to mid-fall
- ↔ 2–5in (5–13cm)
- ★★ Small space rating

Varieties to try
'Kelvedon Wonder' Dwarf early or main crop variety with small peas.
'Snow Wind' Snow pea variety, almost leafless, with sweet pods.
'Sugar Ann' A sugar snap pea with pale, succulent pods.
How to grow Sow seed under cover, 1½in (4cm) deep, into cardboard tubes or biodegradable pots to avoid disturbing their roots when planting out. Seed can also be sown directly outdoors in single or double rows, 2–5in (5–13cm) apart. Support taller varieties with poles, a trellis, or netting, and mulch young plants to retain moisture. Keep plants well watered once in flower and as the pods swell, and crop regularly to encourage a prolonged harvest.

GREEN BEANS

- ☀ Full sun or part shade
- ⧗ 10–16 weeks
- ⌂ Mid-spring to midsummer
- ⚐ Late spring to early summer
- ⚘ Late spring to midsummer
- ◖ Midsummer to fall
- ↔ 2–4in (5–10cm)
- ★★★ Small space rating

Varieties to try
'Kentucky Wonder' Bright green, stringless pods with plump seeds.
'Cobra' Stringless green beans with mauve flowers.
'Roquencourt' Dwarf variety with yellow pods.
How to grow Sow seed undercover, two per 4in (10cm) pot, harden them off, and plant outside after the risk of frost has passed. Climbing varieties will require support. Seed can also be sown outside after the last frost. Sow 2–3 seeds at the base of each support, and protect them against slugs. Tie in the stems as they grow, then pinch off their tips when they reach the top of their support. Harvest the beans regularly, while they are young and tender, to encourage a larger harvest.

RUNNER BEANS

- ☀ Full sun or part shade
- ⧗ 10–16 weeks
- ⌂ Mid-spring to midsummer
- ⚐ Late spring to early summer
- ⚘ Late spring to midsummer
- ◖ Midsummer to fall
- ↔ 6in (15cm)
- ★★★ Small space rating

Varieties to try
'St. George' Good cropper with red and white flowers.
'Polestar' Stringless and tasty variety with bright red flowers.
'Sunset' Reliable cropper with attractive apricot flowers.
How to grow Vigorous but also tender, so sow under cover, two seeds per 4in (10cm) pot. Harden the seedlings off and plant out after the risk of frost has passed, when seed can also be sown directly outside. Provide a tall support of poles or netting, and tie in new growth until plants start to climb themselves. Earlier flowers may not be pollinated if the weather is too cold for bees, and will fail to fruit. Sow batches 3–4 weeks apart for beans throughout the whole summer.

BROAD BEANS

- ☀ Full sun
- ⧗ 12–28 weeks
- ⌂ Late winter to mid-spring
- ⚐ Early spring to late spring
- ⚘ Late winter to mid-spring
- ◖ Late spring to late summer
- ↔ 10in (25cm)
- ★ Small space rating

Varieties to try
'Windsor Bush' Buttery flavor and smooth texture.
'Stereo' Thin-skinned pods that can be eaten whole.
'The Sutton' Dwarf variety with nutty, white beans.
How to grow Broad beans have long roots, so sow them singly in long tubes under cover, or in deep beds of rich, free-draining soil outside. Early crops can be sown in fall, but since they will not stand waterlogging or cold winters, protect those sown outdoors with cloches or fabric. Water well during flowering for a bigger crop. When the first beans appear, pinch off the tops to encourage the pods to grow, and to deter aphids. Pick regularly while the pods are tender.

RADISHES

- ☀ Full sun or part shade
- ⧗ 2–8 weeks (summer); 8–10 weeks (winter)
- ⌂ Midwinter to early spring
- ⚐ Mid-spring
- ⚘ Mid- to late spring
- ◖ Late spring to midwinter
- ↔ ½in (1cm) summer; 9in (23cm) winter
- ★★★ Small space rating

Varieties to try
'Mino Early' Winter radish with long, white, tapering roots.
'Pink Beauty' Summer type with sweet, pink-skinned roots.
'Scarlet Globe' Bright red summer radish with round roots.
How to grow Summer radishes grow rapidly, producing small roots to eat raw in salads. The roots soon become tough, so sow batches every 2–3 weeks, even using them to fill gaps between larger crops. Early crops can be sown indoors, ready to plant out once the risk of frost has passed. Later sowings can be made outside. Winter radishes are large and slow growing, and are eaten cooked. Sow them thinly outdoors from mid- to late summer, thinning them to 9in (23cm) apart.

CARROTS

☀ Full sun or part shade
⧗ 12–20 weeks
⌂ Not applicable
🌱 Mid-spring to late spring
🍴 n/a
👐 Late spring to early winter
↔ 2–4in (5–10cm)
★★ Small space rating

Varieties to try
'Bangor' Main crop carrot with smooth skins that store well.
'Sugarsnax 54' Bright orange, long roots with a very sweet flavor.
'Parmex' Round, sweet baby carrots that crop early.
How to grow Choose round-rooted varieties for containers, and those with long roots for beds, which can also be harvested early as baby roots. Sow seed thinly, where they are to grow, in containers and beds, and them keep moist to encourage germination. For spring crops, sow fall to winter; sow throughout spring and summer for later harvests. Protect early crops from frost using fabric, and install fine netting to deter carrot rust fly larvae that attack the roots.

BEETS

☀ Full sun or part shade
⧗ 8–12 weeks
⌂ Early spring
🌱 Mid-spring to summer
🍴 Mid-spring to midsummer
👐 Midsummer to fall
↔ 2–4in (5–10cm)
★★★ Small space rating

Varieties to try
'Chioggia' Round-rooted with striped pink and white flesh.
'Boltardy' This reliable variety is resistant to bolting.
'Burpees Golden' This variety has distinctive yellow roots.
How to grow Seeds can be sown directly outdoors from mid-spring, and also in cell packs to plant into any available space. Sow every few weeks and harvest the roots throughout summer and fall. Each seed capsule actually contains up to five individual seeds, so thin out the seedlings to leave one strong plant, spaced 4in (10cm) apart. Plants spaced more closely can be harvested as baby roots; farther apart for larger, mature roots. The foliage is edible and can be lightly picked.

POTATOES

☀ Full sun
⧗ 12–22 weeks
⌂ n/a
🌱 n/a
🍴 Spring
👐 Early summer to mid-fall
↔ 12–16in (30–40cm)
★ Small space rating

Varieties to try
'Charlotte' A salad potato with waxy yellow flesh.
'Adirondack Red' Beautiful red flesh and great taste.
'Elba' Impressive round white potato with good disease resistance.
How to grow Potatoes are referred to as early, main, and storage types, according to when they mature. All can be grown in containers and raised beds. Earlier types mature first, so are best for small spaces. Plant seed tubers into rich soil, or in 6in (15cm) of soil mix at the base of a large container. Protect young shoots of early crops from frost. As the stems grow, pile soil at their base to within 4in (10cm) of their tips. Do this 2–3 times to prevent green potatoes.

TURNIPS

☀ Full sun or part shade
⧗ 6–10 weeks
⌂ Late winter to early spring
🌱 Early spring to mid-spring
🍴 Early spring to late summer
👐 Late spring to early winter
↔ 3–5in (8–13cm)
★★ Small space rating

Varieties to try
'Golden Ball' A yellow-skinned variety with a mild flavor.
'Ivory' Very early cropper with sweet-tasting white roots.
'Primera' Best pulled young, it has sweet, purple-tinged white roots.
How to grow For early crops, sow indoors in cell packs and thin to one per cell, harden them off, and plant out once seedlings are large enough to handle. Alternatively, sow direct every 2–3 weeks from early spring for a constant supply. Because turnips prefer cool, moist conditions, keep those sown in summer well watered and shaded. Dry plants can become woody. Harvest turnips once they reach golf ball size. Eat them raw or cooked, and use the thinnings in salads.

LEEKS

- ☀ Full sun or part shade
- ⏳ 30–32 weeks
- ❄ Mid- to late winter
- 🌱 Mid-spring to midsummer
- ⚘ Early to mid-spring
- 🍲 Late summer to mid-spring
- ↔ 6–8in (15–20cm)
- ★★ Small space rating

Varieties to try

'Oarsman F1' Midseason variety with good rust and bolting tolerance.
'King Richard' Grown as an early baby leek, it has long, slim stems.
'Toledo' This late season leek is bolt resistant with long stems.

How to grow Leeks are easily transplanted, so can be sown in seedbeds or indoors to save space while they develop. Sow thinly in small pots or cell packs in winter, or in a seedbed once the soil is workable, early to mid-spring. Plant out seedlings when pencil-thick and 8in (20cm) tall. Make 6in (15cm) deep planting holes, drop a leek into each one. Do not fill the hole with soil, just water the plants well. As they grow, pile earth around the stems to blanch and support them.

KOHLRABI

- ☀ Full sun or part shade
- ⏳ 9–12 weeks
- ❄ Early spring
- 🌱 Late spring
- ⚘ Mid- to late spring
- 🍲 Summer to fall
- ↔ 10in (25cm)
- ★★★ Small space rating

Varieties to try

'Purple Danube' This purple variety has sweet-tasting bulbs.
'Quickstar' A pale, green-skinned variety that is bolt resistant.
'Logo' Ideal for baby bulbs, this is a green-skinned variety.

How to grow For early bulbs, sow indoors into cell packs in early spring, and plant out about 6 weeks later when the soil is warmer. For a succession of crops, sow directly outdoors every few weeks from mid-spring, thinning to 10in (25cm) apart, and harvest when the size of a tennis ball. For mini kohlrabi, thin to 2in (5cm) apart, and harvest when the size of a golf ball. Kohlrabi is a member of the brassica family—don't sow it where other brassicas have been recently grown.

FLORENCE FENNEL

- ☀ Full sun
- ⏳ 8–24 weeks
- ❄ Mid-spring
- 🌱 Late spring
- ⚘ Late spring
- 🍲 Summer to early fall
- ↔ 12in (30cm)
- ★ Small space rating

Varieties to try

'Cantino' This variety has good bolt resistance.
'Zefa Fino' Produces large flattened bulbs with a good flavor.
'Romanesco' A traditional variety with tasty and tender stems.

How to grow Sow seed in large cell packs or 4in (10cm) pots indoors, 4–6 weeks before the last frost, then plant them out in a warm and sheltered spot. Alternatively, sow seed directly in the soil during early summer for a later crop. Florence fennel can be tricky to grow, because fluctuations in temperature or a lack of water can cause the plants to bolt (flower suddenly), leading to poor bulb development. To prevent bolting, keep your plants moist at all times.

GREEN ONIONS

- ☀ Full sun
- ⏳ 10–14 weeks
- ❄ Early to mid-spring
- 🌱 Late spring to early fall
- ⚘ Early summer
- 🍲 Midsummer to mid-fall
- ↔ ½in (1cm)
- ★★ Small space rating

Varieties to try

'Deep Purple' This variety has a round violet bulbs and green leaves.
'Laser' Slow to form bulbs, this vigorous variety has a mild flavor.
'Lisbon' This traditional variety is good in containers.

How to grow For a constant supply in summer, sow directly outdoors every two weeks from late spring, protecting them from frost. Thin seedlings to ½in (1cm) apart, keep them watered to keep the stems from becoming bulbous, and harvest when they reach a usable size. For plants to overwinter until spring, sow seed in late summer. Ideal for containers, you can even sow them in pots on a warm, bright windowsill during winter; thin to 4–5 seedlings per 4in (10cm) pot.

GARLIC

- ☀ Full sun
- ⧗ 20–36 weeks
- ⌂ n/a
- ⚘ n/a
- �} Mid-fall to early spring
- ♨ Late spring to early fall
- ↔ 8in (20cm)
- ★ Small space rating

Varieties to try

'Germidour' A mild variety with purple-streaked skins.
'Solent White' Forms large, white, tasty bulbs that store well.
'German Red' Full-bodied, strong, and spicy with easy-to-peel cloves.
How to grow Requiring a cold period to mature, this crop can be grown through winter when beds or containers are empty. Plant cloves directly from mid-fall to late winter in well drained soil, with their tips showing above the soil surface. Lift them once their leaves yellow in late spring or early summer. Or, plant in early spring to mature from midsummer. You can also plant cloves indoors in pots in early spring if conditions are very wet, for planting out in mid-spring.

CHICORY

- ☀ Full sun or part shade
- ⧗ 10–16 weeks
- ⌂ Early spring and fall to winter
- ⚘ Early summer
- �} Summer
- ♨ Midsummer to late winter
- ↔ 12in (30cm)
- ★★ Small space rating

Varieties to try

'Palla Rossa' A bolt-resistant radicchio with dense red hearts.
'Pan di Zucchero' Sugarloaf type, ideal as a cut-and-come-again.
'Rossa di Treviso Precoce' A radicchio ideal for winter harvesting.
How to grow Red chicory, or radicchio, and green sugarloaf types are grown in a similar way to lettuce but are hardier. Seed can be started early under cover during spring, ready to plant out in summer, or sown directly in summer. Plant or thin out the seedlings to about 12in (30cm) apart. Seed can also be sown under cover during fall and winter, with the plants grown under protection as a cut-and-come-again crop. Water plants well to prevent bolting.

LETTUCE

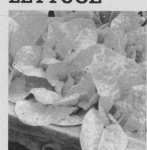

- ☀ Full sun or part shade
- ⧗ 9–12 weeks
- ⌂ Early spring
- ⚘ Mid-spring to late summer
- �} Mid-spring to late summer
- ♨ Midsummer to fall
- ↔ 6–14in (15–35cm)
- ★★★ Small space rating

Varieties to try

'Cocarde' An oak-leaf variety with upright heads.
'Freckles' Romaine lettuce with red-speckled green leaves.
'Maravilla de Verano Canasta' Crisp and green with red tips.
How to grow Sow early crops under cover in spring into cell packs, thinning each cell to a single plant. Harden off and plant out once large enough to handle. From mid-spring onward, sow seed directly. If the weather is hot, however, wait until evening, since lettuce will not germinate in temperatures above 77°F (25°C). Thin seedlings, using the thinnings in salads. Harvest by picking the outer leaves or cut the whole head near the base, leaving the stump to resprout.

SPINACH

- ☀ Part shade
- ⧗ 6–12 weeks
- ⌂ n/a
- ⚘ Late spring to early fall
- �} n/a
- ♨ Mid-spring to late fall
- ↔ 6in (15cm)
- ★★ Small space rating

Varieties to try

'Barbados' This upright variety has smooth, rounded leaves.
'Medania' A prolific variety with soft, deep green leaves.
'Monnopa' Bolt resistant, its thick leaves are sweet tasting.
How to grow Plants sown indoors tend to bolt, so sow directly outdoors every three weeks for a succession of leaves. Thin the seedlings to 3in (8cm) apart, then remove alternate plants to use as young leaves and let the remainder mature. Leave late summer and early fall sowings to overwinter for early crops next year. Water this fast-growing leaf crop regularly to prevent bolting. Harvest young leaves for salads from six weeks and mature spinach after ten weeks.

MUSTARD GREENS

- ☀ Full sun or part shade
- ⏳ 6–8 weeks
- 🏠 Late spring to early summer
- 🌱 Mid- to late summer
- 🌿 Mid- to late summer
- 🖐 Midsummer to late fall
- ↔ 6–12in (15–30cm)
- ★★★ Small space rating

Varieties to try
'Golden Streaks' The frilly lime green leaves have a sweet flavor.
'Green-in-the-snow' Its jagged leaves have a peppery taste.
'Red Giant' This variety has broad, purple-tinted green leaves.
How to grow Mustard greens are full of vitamins, taste spicier as they mature, and are great in salads and stir fries. To keep plants from bolting in cool conditions early in the season, sow seed under cover in cell packs, and plant out when the seedlings are large enough to handle. From midsummer, sow directly, using any thinnings as a baby leaf crop. Pick individual leaves or cut the entire head off at the base. Alternatively, sow closely and harvest as a cut-and-come-again crop

ARUGULA

- ☀ Full sun or part shade
- ⏳ 4–12 weeks
- 🏠 Spring and early fall
- 🌱 Late spring and mid-fall
- 🌿 Mid-spring to mid-fall
- 🖐 Early spring to early winter
- ↔ 6in (15cm)
- ★★★ Small space rating

Varieties to try
'Apollo' Best eaten young, it has large, rounded dark green leaves.
'Pegasus' Mildly peppery, its leaves are large and serrated.
'Sky Rocket' This variety is fast growing and slow to bolt.
How to grow Prone to bolting in hot or dry conditions, and with age, repeat sow for a continuous supply of tender leaves. Sow a new batch once previous seedlings have two true leaves—every 2–3 weeks, depending on the weather. Sow directly outdoors or, in cool areas, sow indoors during spring and fall into containers, protecting them with fabric. Keep well watered and harvest after two weeks as a cut-and-come-again crop, or pick whole plants after four weeks.

SWISS CHARD

- ☀ Full sun or part shade
- ⏳ 8–16 weeks
- 🏠 Early to mid-spring
- 🌱 Mid-spring to late summer
- 🌿 Late spring to early summer
- 🖐 Midsummer to spring
- ↔ 8–15in (20–38cm)
- ★★★ Small space rating

Varieties to try
'Bright Lights' Provides a mixture of brightly colored stems.
'Charlotte' Resistant to bolting, this variety has bright red stems.
'Fordhook Giant' A large-leaf type with crisp white stems.
How to grow Swiss chard can be cropped for its young tender leaves in summer, or grown over fall and winter to provide mature stems and leaves for steaming. Sow seed thinly directly into the soil or in cell packs. Each pod contains a number of seeds, so thin to one plant per sowing location. Sow in spring for a summer harvest, thinning plants to 8in (20cm) apart. For fall and winter crops, sow in late summer, thinning the plants out to 15in (38cm) apart.

BOK CHOY

- ☀ Full sun
- ⏳ 5–10 weeks
- 🏠 Mid-spring to early summer
- 🌱 Midsummer to late summer
- 🌿 Late spring to early summer
- 🖐 Early summer to mid-fall
- ↔ 4–10in (10–25cm)
- ★★★ Small space rating

Varieties to try
'Choko' This variety has slender green leaves.
'Glacier' Bolt resistant, it has white stems and white-veined leaves.
'Joi Choi' A white-stemmed variety, it resists bolting.
How to grow A useful catch crop, this fast-growing brassica is tasty at all stages, from early thinnings to plump mature heads. Prone to bolting if they become too hot, cold, or dry, sow bolt-resistant varieties indoors in spring at 50–55°F (10–13°C). Sow seed singly and transplant as soon as seedlings can be handled. In summer, sow seed directly outside, thinning to 4in (10cm) apart for baby cut-and-come-again leaves, or 10in (25cm) for mature heads. Water plants regularly.

ENDIVE

- ☼ Full sun or part shade
- ⧗ 12–14 weeks
- 🏠 Mid- to late spring
- 🌱 Early summer to midsummer
- 🍴 Early summer to late summer
- 🥬 Midsummer to late fall
- ↔ 10in (25cm)
- ★★ Small space rating

Varieties to try
'Frenzy' A frisée-type with compact, self-blanching heads.
'Natacha' Bolt-resistant, Batavian variety with broad leaves.
'Pancalieri' A mild, self-blanching, bolt-resistant frisée variety.
How to grow Endive comes in two types, frisée types with frilly leaves, and the hardier Batavian types with rounded leaves. For a continuous supply, sow a batch every few weeks. Start by sowing indoors in spring to prevent bolting, harden off the seedlings, and plant out once it is warmer. In summer, sow seed directly outside. Once the heads are large enough, cover them with a plate, or tie them closed using string for ten days to reduce their bitter flavor.

SWEET CORN

- ☼ Full sun
- ⧗ 16–24 weeks
- 🏠 Mid- to late spring
- 🌱 Early summer
- 🍴 Late spring to early summer
- 🥬 Late summer to mid-fall
- ↔ 14–18in (35–45cm) in a block
- ★ Small space rating

Varieties to try
'Minipop F1' A baby corn, picked young, and ideal for small spaces.
'Ovation' This is a midseason variety with large, sweet cobs.
'Swift' Dwarf variety, suitable for cool areas. It matures early.
How to grow Sweet corn is wind-pollinated, so is grown in blocks, and can be underplanted with lower-growing crops, such as lettuce. It needs warmth to germinate and a long growing season. Sow indoors singly in tubes or deep cell packs in spring to plant out in early summer. In early summer, seed can be sown directly in pairs, then thinned to leave the strongest plants. Support the tall stems with poles. Water well when plants are flowering and the cobs form.

KALE

- ☼ Full sun or part shade
- ⧗ 14–32 weeks
- 🏠 Mid- to late spring
- 🌱 Early summer
- 🍴 Late spring to midsummer
- 🥬 Fall to the following spring
- ↔ 24in (60cm)
- ★★ Small space rating

Varieties to try
'Cavolo Nero' This variety has slender, dark green, crinkly leaves.
'Redbor' An attractive variety with frilly leaves and purple stems.
'Red Russian' Grown for its serrated gray leaves and purple stems.
How to grow Kale grown for winter cropping can take up a lot of space, so sow in individual pots in mid- to late spring, and plant out in their final locations in midsummer, as space becomes available. Keep plants well watered and provide support as they grow. Kale can be harvested in fall and winter by picking the outer leaves, leaving the inner ones to grow. They can also be harvested as baby leaves during summer and treated as a cut-and-come-again crop.

SPROUTING BROCCOLI

- ☼ Full sun
- ⧗ 34–38 weeks
- 🏠 Late spring
- 🌱 Early summer
- 🍴 Midsummer
- 🥬 Late winter to late spring
- ↔ 24in (60cm)
- ★ Small space rating

Varieties to try
'Red Arrow' This variety is an early cropper, ready to pick in winter.
'Claret' Cropping in spring, this variety matures later.
'Italian Green Sprouting' With 5–8in heads and many sideshoots.
How to grow These are large plants that fill the hungry gap from winter to spring. Sow in individual pots or cell packs, ½in (1cm) deep in late spring, and plant out firmly when space becomes available in midsummer. Seed can also be sown directly outside in early summer, ready to transplant into their final locations. Net young plants to deter birds, keep them well watered, and provide support as they grow. In summer, underplant with lettuce and other low-growing crops.

ALPINE STRAWBERRIES

- ☀ Full sun or part shade
- ✕ Every summer once established
- ⌂ Spring or fall
- ⊟ Late spring
- ⚑ Mid-spring or early fall
- ❥ Summer
- ↔ 12–15in (30–40cm)
- ★★ Small space rating

Varieties to try

'Alexandra' This compact variety is quick to fruit from seed.
'Baron Solemacher' Ideal for containers, it bears dark red fruit.
'Regina' This variety bears masses of large, sweet, scarlet berries.
How to grow These perennials self-seed readily, yield a few dainty
fruit at a time, and make good groundcover. Sow seed under cover in
spring, grow the seedlings on in pots, then plant them out once the
risk of frost has passed. You can also sow directly in rows, but protect
seedlings from slugs. Avoid getting the fruit wet, which causes them
to rot. Remove runners for the best fruit, but propagate fresh plants
from runners every 3–4 years. The tiny white flowers are also edible.

STRAWBERRIES

- ☀ Full sun
- ✕ Every summer once established
- ⌂ n/a
- ⊟ n/a
- ⚑ Spring or fall
- ❥ Early summer to early fall
- ↔ 12–16in (30–40cm)
- ★★ Small space rating

Varieties to try

'Eversweet Everbearer' Fruits throughout spring, summer, and fall.
'Honeoye' Consistently bears heavy yields of large, crimson fruit.
'Elegance' Garden variety producing enormous, tasty strawberries.
How to grow These perennials are usually grown from bare-root
or pot-grown plants. There are two types: summer-bearers, which
produce a single flush of fruit in early to midsummer, and everbearing
types that fruit mainly in summer, then sporadically into fall. Plant
outdoors into rich soil or in containers, spacing container plants 6in
(15cm) apart. Water well and feed with tomato fertilizer, and keep
the fruit off the soil surface using plastic sheeting or dry straw.

RASPBERRIES

- ☀ Full sun or part shade
- ✕ Every fall once established
- ⌂ n/a
- ⊟ n/a
- ⚑ Late fall to early spring
- ❥ Late summer to mid-fall
- ↔ 14–18in (35–45cm)
- ★★★ Small space rating

Varieties to try

'All Gold' Bears fragrant, amber berries on self-supporting canes.
'Autumn Bliss' This variety gives good crops of large red berries.
'Polka' Early and free fruiting, its canes are almost thornless.
How to grow Available as bare-root or container-grown plants,
they can be grown directly in the soil or in large containers.
Raspberries generally don't need support, and crop on the current
season's growth. In spring, mulch to retain soil moisture, then water
and feed well for the most successful fruiting. Net plants to protect
the berries from birds, and harvest the fruit until the first frost. Cut
down the canes to ground level in late winter.

JAPANESE WINEBERRIES

- ☀ Sun or part shade
- ✕ Every summer once established
- ⌂ n/a
- ⊟ n/a
- ⚑ Fall to early spring
- ❥ Mid- to late summer
- ↔ 8–11ft (2.5–3.5m)
- ★★ Small space rating

Varieties to try

None available—Only the species is grown.
How to grow This is a vigorous shrub that can be planted directly
into rich soil, or grown in a large container. Since wineberries fruit on
stems produced the previous year, you'll have to wait at least 18
months for your first berries. When pruned correctly, however, they
then fruit every summer. Keep plants well watered, especially when
fruiting, and tie in their pink, fuzzy stems to a support, such as a trellis
or a cane tepee. To restrict their size in small spaces, train the stems
into figure eights, looping them around themselves. Once fruited, cut
out the old stems and tie in the new ones to fruit next year.

BLACKBERRIES

- ☀ Full sun or part shade
- ⊠ Every summer once established
- ⌂ n/a
- ⚬ n/a
- ⚘ Fall to early spring
- ⚫ Midsummer to early fall
- ↔ 8–11ft (2.5–3.5m)
- ★★ Small space rating

Varieties to try
'Loch Ness' Compact and thornless, it bears large, sweet fruit.
'Silvan' An early variety with large, long, purple-black fruit.
'Waldo' Thornless and compact, this is ideal for containers.
How to grow Blackberries fruit freely on long, clambering stems, although there are compact, thornless varieties available, suitable for large containers. To provide support, plant them against horizontal wires fixed to a fence or between two posts. As fruit is borne on two-year-old canes, train the canes into a fan shape in the first year, then, after fruiting in the second, cut them to the base, retaining the new stems to fruit the following year. Water and feed as per raspberries.

BLUEBERRIES

- ☀ Full sun or part shade
- ⊠ Every summer once established
- ⌂ n/a
- ⚬ n/a
- ⚘ Fall to early spring
- ⚫ Late summer to early fall
- ↔ 5ft (1.5m)
- ★ Small space rating

Varieties to try
'Duke' This is an early and free-fruiting variety.
'Spartan' With an upright form, it bears richly flavored fruit.
'Top Hat' A dwarf variety with small and sweet, bright blue berries.
How to grow Ideal for containers, blueberries produce masses of berries, as well as having attractive spring flowers and bright fall foliage. They must be grown in free-draining acidic soil, and should be kept moist at all times using rainwater (tap water is often alkaline). For the best crop, grow two plants, so they can pollinate each other. Mulch in spring and net against birds. After two years, prune each spring, removing congested growth, plus one or two older stems.

APPLES

- ☀ Full sun
- ⊠ Every summer once established
- ⌂ n/a
- ⚬ n/a
- ⚘ Fall to early spring
- ⚫ Midsummer to mid-fall
- ↔ 6–12ft (1.8–3.6m)
- ★ Small space rating

Varieties to try
'Cox's Orange Pippin' A self-pollinating apple for eating or cooking.
'Ben Davis' Dependable producer that bears firm, juicy fruit.
'Liberty' Crisp white flesh and sweet-tart taste perfect for fresh eating.
How to grow For small spaces and containers, choose apples grafted onto dwarfing rootstock M26, and consider training them into space-saving shapes, such as a fan, cordon, or espalier. To ensure the flowers are pollinated and set fruit, grow two trees, unless there is another nearby. Stake freestanding trees, and water well until they are established. Remove fruit in the first year, thereafter thin them to get fewer, but bigger, apples. Depending on type, prune summer or winter.

PEARS

- ☀ Full sun
- ⊠ Every summer once established
- ⌂ n/a
- ⚬ n/a
- ⚘ Fall to early spring
- ⚫ Late summer to mid-fall
- ↔ 6–12ft (1.8–3.6m)
- ★ Small space rating

Varieties to try
'Concorde' Compact and self-pollinating, with long dessert pears.
'Doyenné du Comice' Bears sweet, juicy, large fruit.
'Luscious' A blushing, sweet yellow dessert pear.
How to grow Like apples, choose trees on dwarfing rootstocks and prune them into space-saving shapes. You can also choose varieties specially grown for use in containers. Pears require a warm spot and protection from frost to fruit well; they also need one or two pollinating partners, so seek advice on suitable varieties. Stake freestanding trees or train in to their supports. Mulch in spring, thin the fruit, and water well in summer. Depending on the type, prune in summer or winter.

FRENCH SORREL

- ☀ Part shade
- ⌛ 8–18 weeks
- 🌱 Early to mid-spring
- 🪴 Late spring
- 🌿 Mid- to late spring
- 🥄 Summer to fall
- ↔ 12in (30cm)
- ★★★ Small space rating

Varieties to try
'De Belleville' This has pale green leaves with a lemony flavor.
'Silver Shield' Forms low mat of silvery green, spear-shaped leaves.
How to grow This hardy perennial adds a lemon or apple tartness to salads, as well as egg, cheese, and fish dishes. Sow batches thinly into cell packs indoors, or direct outdoors, and thin when the seedlings are large enough to handle. Mulch and water well to keep the soil moist and cool to stop the leaves from becoming bitter. Pick young leaves before flowering. Remove the flowers to stop the plants from seeding and becoming invasive. Cover in winter and continue to pick the leaves. Established plants can be divided in spring or fall.

LOVAGE

- ☀ Full sun or part shade
- ⌛ 42–60 weeks
- 🌱 Late winter to late spring
- 🪴 Mid-spring to early summer
- 🌿 Spring to summer, or in fall
- 🥄 Late spring to early winter
- ↔ 24in (60cm)
- ★★★ Small space rating

Varieties to try
None available—Only the species is grown.
How to grow This hardy perennial reaches 6ft (2m) tall, providing celery-flavored leaves that may be used like spinach in salads, stews, and soups. New plants need time to establish before being picked. Either plant container grown plants in fall to pick the following year or, if sowing from seed, only harvest from them in their second season. Sow indoors in cell packs or direct in rows outside. Pick young, tender leaves early in the season before the flowers appear. Keep the plants moist and cut back in fall. You can divide mature plants in spring. Note: Eating large amounts may cause stomach upset.

PARSLEY

- ☀ Full sun or part shade
- ⌛ 8–12 weeks
- 🌱 Early spring and early fall
- 🪴 Late spring to early summer
- 🌿 Late spring to late summer
- 🥄 Year-round
- ↔ 6in (15cm)
- ★★ Small space rating

Varieties to try
'Laura' A flat-leaf variety with a more intense flavor.
'Lisette' Curly-leaf parsley with bright green, sweet foliage.
'Titan' Flat-leaf variety with lacy, dark green leaves.
How to grow Usually grown as an annual, if sown in regular batches, it can be harvested all year. Sow indoors in spring into cell packs to avoid root disturbance, keep at a steady 64°F (18°C), and plant out once the risk of frost has passed. In summer, sow directly into moist soil. Keep plants moist, feed weekly with a high-nitrogen fertilizer, and remove any flowers that appear. Late-sown seedlings can be potted and grown indoors on a bright windowsill.

SWEET CICELY

- ☀ Part shade
- ⌛ 16–20 weeks
- 🌱 n/a
- 🪴 Mid-fall to late winter
- 🌿 Late winter to fall
- 🥄 Spring and summer
- ↔ 20–24in (50–60cm)
- ★★★ Small space rating

Varieties to try
None available—Only the species is grown.
How to grow The ferny leaves of this herb have a sweet, aniseed scent, which is great in salads or fruit desserts. It is a large, very hardy perennial, and its seeds need cold to germinate. Sow singly in pots or cell packs, and leave them outside over winter to germinate in spring, or sow seed directly, thinning to leave the strongest plants. Harvest leaves regularly and remove the flat, white flowerheads in summer for new flushes of foliage. You could allow it to flower—stop picking leaves while it does—and use the unripe seeds to add a sharp aniseed tang to salads. Don't allow the seeds to fall. It self-seeds very readily.

FENNEL

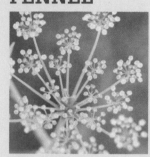

☀ Full sun
⧗ 16–20 weeks
⌂ Early- to mid-spring
🌱 Late spring to early summer
🌿 Late spring
🍃 Early summer to mid-fall
↔ 18in (45cm)
★★★ Small space rating

Varieties to try
Foeniculum vulgare Has green foliage and flat yellow flowerheads.
'Purpureum' This variety has bronze foliage, maturing to gray-green.
How to grow This elegant herb has aniseed-flavored feathery
fronds, stems, and seeds. It can be grown as an annual for its leaves,
sowing the seeds directly in spring, or as a perennial for its young
leaves and flavorful seeds. To grow it as a perennial, sow indoors in
spring into cell packs to avoid disturbing the long taproot, then plant
out once the risk of frost has passed. Pick leaves regularly before
plants flower, or to prolong the harvest, remove the flowering stems.
Harvest seed in late summer. Mature plants can be lifted and divided.

STARFLOWER

☀ Full sun
⧗ 10–14 weeks
⌂ Early spring
🌱 Mid- to late spring
🌿 Mid- to late spring
🍃 Early summer to early fall
↔ 8in (20cm)
★★★ Small space rating

Varieties to try
Borago officinalis Blue-flowered with large, fuzzy, gray-green leaves.
'Alba' This variety has white flowers and large green, fuzzy leaves.
How to grow Borage is grown for its edible flowers, which can be
added to summer drinks, ice cubes, salads, and desserts. The leaves
can also be picked when young and used in salads. Sow seed indoors
in pots or cell packs in spring, harden off, and plant out when large
enough to handle, so as not to disturb their taproots. Seed can also
be sown directly and thinned. It is best grown in poor soil or soil mix
to keep it from getting leggy. Pick the flowers regularly to keep new
buds forming into fall. Don't allow it to set seed—it spreads rapidly.

SAGE

☀ Full sun
⧗ All year once established
⌂ n/a
🌱 n/a
🌿 Fall and spring
🍃 Year-round
↔ 16in (40cm)
★★ Small space rating

Varieties to try
'Albiflora' This has spikes of white flowers and gray-green leaves.
'Icterina' An attractive shrub with gold variegated foliage.
'Purpurascens' Semievergreen with purple-green leaves.
How to grow This shrubby perennial is a classic herb, and one
plant will provide a year-round supply of aromatic leaves, to use fresh
or dried. It is best bought as a container-grown plant, and requires
light, free-draining soil or potting mix. Pick the leaves regularly, which
taste milder before flowering and stronger afterward. Prune plants
after flowering into a neat shape and for new growth. After 3–4 years,
sage is best replaced. Buy a new plant or take cuttings in summer.

LAVENDER

☀ Full sun
⧗ Every summer once established
⌂ n/a
🌱 n/a
🌿 Fall or spring
🍃 Early summer to mid-fall
↔ 16–20in (40–50cm)
★★ Small space rating

Varieties to try
'Hidcote' This has dark violet flowers and silvery gray foliage.
'Loddon Pink' Compact with short, grayish-pink flower spikes.
'Munstead' A dwarf plant, with gray leaves and deep blue flowers.
How to grow The highly aromatic leaves and flowers may be used
sparingly to flavor sugar, desserts, cookies, cakes, teas, and oils. Best
bought in spring as plugs or container-grown plants, lavender requires
free-draining soil or potting mix. Harvest the flowers during summer
and the leaves into fall. After flowering, shear off all flowered stems,
but do not cut into old wood, as it does not resprout. Lavender plants
can be short-lived and may need replacing after 4–5 years.

ROSEMARY

- ☀ Full sun
- ⊠ All year once established
- n/a
- n/a
- 🌱 Late spring
- 🍴 Year-round
- ↔ 16in (40cm)
- ★★ Small space rating

Varieties to try
'Green Ginger' Compact and upright with ginger-scented leaves.
'Miss Jessopp's Upright' Has silvery foliage and blue spring flowers.
'Roseus' A pink-flowered variety with bright green foliage.
How to grow An evergreen shrub, rosemary provides a year-round supply of leaves once mature; spring and early summer leaves are more tender. Young plants and some varieties are not fully hardy, so wait until all risk of frost has passed before planting it outdoors into well drained soil or potting mix. In cold and exposed areas, plant it in pots that can be brought under cover for winter. Cut back after flowering in spring or summer to keep it neat and to prompt new growth.

BASIL

- ☀ Full sun
- ⊠ 6–8 weeks
- Early spring to early summer
- Early to midsummer
- 🌱 Early to midsummer
- 🍴 Early summer to fall
- ↔ 10in (25cm)
- ★★★ Small space rating

Varieties to try
'Cinnamon' This has purple-brown foliage with a spicy taste.
'Sweet Green' Ideal for pesto, it has mint- and clove-scented leaves.
'Purple Ruffles' It has strongly flavored, frilly purple-black foliage.
How to grow This tender annual needs hot, dry conditions; it often grows best on a sunny windowsill or under glass. Sow in batches indoors at a minimum of 64°F (18°C), cover thinly, and water seedlings sparingly to avoid rot. Sow in midsummer for plants to last into winter. Sow direct only in warm, sheltered soil or containers. Pick basil tips regularly to keep it compact and producing new leaves. Water plants sparingly and never in the evening—basil hates having a wet base.

AFRICAN BASIL

- ☀ Full sun
- ⊠ 12–28 weeks
- n/a
- n/a
- 🌱 Early summer
- 🍴 Early to late summer
- ↔ 12–16in (30–40cm)
- ★★ Small space rating

Varieties to try
None available—Only the species is grown.
How to grow This herb has deliciously tasty leaves, similar to basil, and its purple spires of flowers are much loved by bees. Unlike traditional basil, it is a tender perennial, and is only available as plugs or container-grown plants, since it does not produce seed. It needs well drained soil or soil mix, and is ideal for containers, although should not be planted out until the risk of frost has passed. Plants can be cut back and brought under cover for winter. To grow new plants, take 4–6in (10–15cm) cuttings during spring. Insert them into gritty soil mix, and water sparingly. They will root in a matter of weeks.

MINT

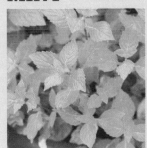

- ☀ Full sun or part shade
- ⊠ Every summer once established
- n/a
- n/a
- 🌱 Mid-spring to early summer
- 🍴 Early to late summer
- ↔ 12–16in (30–40cm)
- ★★★ Small space rating

Varieties to try
Ginger mint (*Mentha* x *gracilis*) It has spicy, variegated leaves.
Spearmint (*M. spicata*) Fresh-tasting leaves with purple flowers.
Apple mint (*M. suaveolens*) Fuzzy green foliage with a zingy taste.
How to grow This is a very useful herb, and one plant of any variety is all you need since they are rampant growers. Buy in spring as a plug or a container-grown plant. All types spread quickly, so they are best grown in large containers, which can be placed into borders to control their spreading roots. Keep plants well watered, pick young leaves regularly, and cut back old stems in summer to encourage new growth. There is a wide range of species and varieties available.

FRENCH TARRAGON

- ☀ Full sun
- ⌛ Every summer once established
- 🌙 n/a
- 🌱 n/a
- 🌿 Spring
- 🍴 Summer to early fall
- ↔ 24in (60cm)
- ★★★ Small space rating

Varieties to try
None available—Only the species is grown.
How to grow This herb has narrow, silver-green leaves that have
a distinctive mint-anise flavor. Difficult to grow from seed in cool
climates, it is best bought as a container-grown plant. It is suitable
for growing in borders or containers, and needs full sun and well
drained, alkaline or neutral soil or potting mix. Tarragon hates cold,
wet conditions, and is not fully hardy, so should be protected from
excessive winter wet and hard frost. Plants grown in containers could
be brought under cover. Although they look similar, do not confuse
this with the more vigorous but less flavorful Russian tarragon.

CHIVES

- ☀ Full sun
- ⌛ Every summer once established
- 🌙 Late winter to late spring
- 🌱 Late spring
- 🌿 Early spring to midsummer
- 🍴 Late spring to mid-fall
- ↔ 6in (15cm)
- ★★★ Small space rating

Varieties to try
'Black Isle Blush' This variety has mauve flowers with pink centers.
'Silver Chimes' A dwarf variety with white flowers. Strongly flavored.
'Forescate' Grown for its pink flowers and tasty blue-green leaves.
How to grow A hardy perennial, chives are a natural cut-and-
come-again crop. Sow indoors thinly in flats, prick out in threes or
fours into pots to grow on, then plant out once frost has passed. Plants
can also be kept under cover for early crops. Seed can also be sown
directly outside in summer. Begin harvesting once the leaves reach
6in (15cm) tall, and cut them back every two months to promote
tender new growth. The attractive flowers are also good to eat.

DILL

- ☀ Full sun
- ⌛ 8–10 weeks
- 🌙 Late winter to early spring
- 🌱 Late spring
- 🌿 Mid-spring to midsummer
- 🍴 Summer
- ↔ 8in (20cm)
- ★★★ Small space rating

Varieties to try
'Bouquet' A dwarf form with highly aromatic, ferny foliage.
'Compatto' Dwarf variety, suitable for containers.
'Dukat' This type has sweetly flavored, blue-green leaves.
How to grow This frost-hardy annual has a long taproot, so grows
best if sown directly. Sow seed outdoors in batches for a constant
supply. Barely cover the seed, and protect early seedlings under
cloches until all risk of frost has passed. For an early crop, sow indoors
in cell packs and thin each to the strongest seedling. Harvest leaves
once plants reach 12in (30cm) tall, cutting the whole plant. You can
also use the edible flowers and seeds. Keep the plants well watered.

MARJORAM

- ☀ Full sun
- ⌛ Every summer once established
- 🌙 n/a
- 🌱 n/a
- 🌿 Late spring to midsummer
- 🍴 Midsummer to mid-fall
- ↔ 10in (25cm)
- ★★★ Small space rating

Varieties to try
'Acorn Bank' A yellow-leaf type with pink flowers.
'Compactum' Forms a low mound of dark green, aromatic leaves.
'Country Cream' Has variegated green and cream foliage.
How to grow A hardy perennial, marjoram is an essential herb in
Mediterranean cooking. Tricky and slow to raise from seed, it is best
bought as plugs or container-grown plants. It is ideal for containers
and window boxes, or to plant alongside a path, and needs full sun
and well drained soil. Harvest the leaves before the flower buds open,
when they taste their best. This herb is often confused with sweet
marjoram, which is less hardy, but still worth growing.

THYME

- ☀ Full sun
- ✕ Every summer once established
- ⌂ n/a
- ⚏ n/a
- ⊥ Late spring to early summer
- ♨ Late spring to early winter
- ↔ 12in (30cm)
- ★★★ Small space rating

Varieties to try
'Golden King' Lemon scented with golden-edged foliage.
'Orange Balsam' Has orange- and thyme-scented leaves.
'Silver Queen' A cream-variegated variety with mauve flowers.
How to grow Evergreen thyme has a creeping style, and is ideal for planting in very small but sunny places. It is slow to grow from seed, so is best bought as container-grown plants. There are many varieties to choose from—some with distinctive flavors. Pick only a few leaves until the plant is established. The flavor is best before flowering; trim plants hard after flowering to prompt fresh growth. Plants require well drained soil and can be short-lived.

CILANTRO

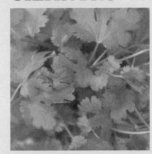

- ☀ Full sun or part shade
- ✕ 4–8 weeks for the leaves
- ⌂ Early spring and fall
- ⚏ Mid-spring
- ⊥ Mid-spring to midsummer
- ♨ Late spring to early winter
- ↔ 10–12in (25–30cm)
- ★★★ Small space rating

Varieties to try
'Calypso' Fast-growing, the leaves can be cut down 3 or 4 times.
'Confetti' This variety has delicate, feathery, sweet-tasting foliage.
'Leisure' Good for containers, it has large, tasty leaves and flowers.
How to grow This annual can be grown in part-shade for the most flavorful leaves, or in full sun for its spicy seeds. Early crops can be sown under cover in spring, although may bolt when planted outside, so seeds are best sown directly outside in monthly batches. Seed can also be sown in pots during fall to grow through winter indoors on a bright windowsill. Cut leaf crops regularly and keep them moist to prevent bolting. Support top-heavy seed crops with poles.

OXALIS TRIANGULARIS

- ☀ Full sun or part shade
- ✕ 8–10 weeks
- ⌂ n/a
- ⚏ n/a
- ⊥ Early summer
- ♨ Midsummer to fall
- ↔ 12in (30cm)
- ★ Small space rating

Varieties to try
None available—only the species is grown
How to grow Often used as a houseplant, this tender perennial can be planted outside for summer, and grown for its lemon-flavored purple leaves and its attractive pale pink flowers. Buy container-grown plants in late spring, and plant them into free-draining soil or potting mix in beds or containers after the last frost. Keep plants well watered and deadhead them frequently to encourage more flowers to grow. Pick the leaves and flowers sparingly, when required, and add them to salads. Plants can be lifted in fall and brought indoors until spring, when larger plants can be divided.

NASTURTIUMS

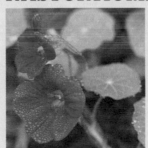

- ☀ Full sun
- ✕ 10–12 weeks
- ⌂ Mid-spring
- ⚏ Late spring to early summer
- ⊥ Late spring and early summer
- ♨ Summer to fall
- ↔ 18in (45cm)
- ★★★ Small space rating

Varieties to try
'Indian Chief' Climber with bright red flowers and dark green leaves.
'Alaska' A variegated type with attractive white-splashed foliage.
'Black Velvet' Bears sumptuous deep red flowers.
How to grow This annual is grown from seed, sown under cover in pots in spring, or directly outside once the risk of frost has passed. It has a trailing or climbing habit, and can be trained up a support or left to creep among your plants. It grows well in most soils, even poor soil, and is suitable for borders and containers. The flowers, leaves, and fresh seeds are all edible, and have a strong peppery taste, especially the seeds. Nasturtiums will self-seed readily.

CALIFORNIA POPPIES

- ☀ Full sun
- ⌛ 10 weeks
- ⌂ n/a
- 🌱 Mid-spring to early summer
- 🌱 n/a
- 🖐 Summer
- ↔ 6–8in (15–20cm)
- ★★★ Small space rating

Varieties to try
'Chrome Queen' Pale yellow flowers with feathery foliage.
'Red Chief' Vibrant red-flowered variety with blue-green leaves.
'Orange King' Has rich orange flowers and feathery leaves.
How to grow The seeds of this annual are sown directly where they are to flower, either in well drained borders or in containers, during mid-spring. Sow in a couple of batches a few weeks apart to extend the flowering season, thinning the seedlings to 6–8in (15–20cm) apart. Pick the flowers as required, adding the petals to salads and summer drinks. Deadhead the plants frequently to encourage repeat flowering. California poppies will readily self-seed, returning year after year.

MARIGOLDS

- ☀ Full sun
- ⌛ 10–12 weeks
- ⌂ Early spring
- 🌱 Mid-spring
- 🌱 Mid- to late spring
- 🖐 Summer to fall
- ↔ 12in (30cm)
- ★★★ Small space rating

Varieties to try
'Neon' This variety has deep orange petals, tipped with red.
'Orange Porcupine' The orange flowers have quilled petals.
'Orange Prince' Free-flowering with open, deep orange flowers.
How to grow This annual is easy to grow from seed, and there are many varieties to try. In early spring, sow seed into small pots or cell packs under cover, and thin the seedlings to leave the strongest. Harden them off and plant out 12in (30cm) apart. Seed can also be sown directly where they are to flower, in borders or containers. Keep plants well watered and deadhead frequently. Marigolds are great for companion planting, and as garnishes in salads and other dishes.

VIOLAS

- ☀ Full sun or part shade
- ⌛ 8–24 weeks
- ⌂ Spring or fall
- 🌱 Late spring
- 🌱 Spring
- 🖐 Summer to early fall
- ↔ 18in (45cm)
- ★★★ Small space rating

Varieties to try
'Heart's ease' (*V. tricolor*) has dainty purple, yellow, and white flowers.
'Pat Kavanagh' This variety has yellow flowers with mauve edges.
'Penny Primrose Picotee' A striking yellow with a purple edge.
How to grow Violas are usually bought as plants, since they are so readily available and cheap to buy. Plant in the garden or in pots in mid- to late spring and, if regularly deadheaded, they should flower throughout summer. Perennial varieties will often flower into fall, and many have a wonderfully sweet scent. Pick the flowers as you need them and add them to salads and summer drinks. Many varieties will self-seed freely, so you may only need to buy them once.

SWEET WILLIAMS

- ☀ Full sun
- ⌛ 32 weeks from plants
- ⌂ n/a
- 🌱 Early to midsummer
- 🌱 Fall
- 🖐 Late spring to early summer
- ↔ 10in (25cm)
- ★★ Small space rating

Varieties to try
'Auricula Eyed' Produces clusters of fringed pink and white flowers.
'Sweet Red' Dwarf form with red flowers that is ideal for containers.
'Diabunda Red Picotee' This variety may bloom in its first year.
How to grow Sweet William is a biennial that is normally bought as year-old plants in fall to flower the following spring. It can also be grown from seeds, which will flower in their second year, although you will need spare space for them to grow in the meantime. Its flowers have a delicious clovelike scent, and can be used to add color to salads and drinks. Keep the plants well watered and deadhead them regularly. Discard spent plants after flowering.

Common pests

Snails and slugs Coming out mostly at night and during wet spells, these pests will attack your crops at every stage of growth, weakening or even killing them. Apply pellets or use slug and snail barriers and traps.

Cabbage white caterpillars Despite their name, these caterpillars feed on most members of the brassica family, stripping their leaves to skeletons. Net plants to stop the adults from laying eggs on your crops.

Carrot rust fly larvae These tiny maggots burrow into the roots of carrots and turnips, creating mush-filled tunnels. Net plants so the adults do not lay eggs near your plants, or grow resistant varieties,

Wireworms Larvae of the click beetle, these soil-dwelling grubs feed on the roots of seedlings, killing them, and burrow into potatoes and onions. There is no treatment. Simply remove the pests if you find them.

Vine weevil grubs These small cream-colored maggots feed on the roots of many crops, especially those grown in containers. Treat containers with a nematode solution and remove any grubs you find in your pots.

Birds Newly planted brassica plants are often stripped of their leaves by birds (*above*). Ripening fruit will also be targeted by many types of birds. Net your plants clear down to soil level to ensure birds cannot sneak below.

Aphids Also known as blackflies or greenflies, these sap-sucking insects form large colonies and can weaken or kill your plants. Treat with insecticide, or wash them off and encourage natural predators.

Cats, dogs, and foxes Whether you like them or not, these can cause significant harm to your crops by digging them up or urinating on them. Use deterrents to keep them away, or protect plants with nets and barriers.

Flea beetle These tiny black beetles, which jump from your plants when disturbed, feed on leaves, especially of seedlings, peppering them with holes. Cover plants with fine fabric as a barrier or use a suitable insecticide.

Pea and bean weevils Creating small notches in the leaves of pea and bean plants, the damage often looks worse than it is. If your plants are weakened, however, treat them using a suitable insecticide.

Cabbage root maggots These small maggots feed on the roots of newly planted members of the brassica family, causing them to wilt and die. Protect seedlings by fitting barrier collars when planting (*above*).

Codling moth caterpillars Attacking apples and pears, these pests burrow into the fruit, creating tunnels, and spoiling them. Lure the egg-laying adults away from your trees using codling moth traps in late spring.

Common diseases and disorders

Blight This fungal disease attacks potatoes, causing brown patches on the leaves, which suddenly wilt, and the tubers may rot. It also affects tomatoes, causing the fruit to turn brown. Infected plants are best discarded.

Blossom end rot A disorder rather than a disease, the ends of tomatoes and zucchini decay, which spreads to the whole fruit. It is caused by erratic watering. Simply water your plants more regularly.

Damping off This fungal disease kills seedlings, most commonly raised indoors, by causing their stems to collapse. To prevent this, sow into new soil mix, water with tapwater, and keep seedlings well ventilated.

Splitting tomato skins This problem results from erratic watering while the fruit are developing. The split fruit may then also rot. Prevent splitting by keeping your plants evenly moist at all times while in fruit.

Clubroot Affecting members of the brassica family, this soilborne disease distorts their roots, causing the plants to wilt and grow weakly—if not die. Grow resistant varieties and rotate your crops annually.

Gray mold This disease affects a wide variety of crops, including fruit. It forms downy gray patches of mold on the leaves, stems, flowers, or fruit, which then decay. Remove affected growth to prevent spread.

Downy mildew Most common in wet weather, the leaves of many crops develop brown patches on the top, with pale mold beneath. Remove infected growth, avoid wetting the leaves, and improve airflow.

Powdery mildew Most common in dry spells when plants are stressed, powdery white patches appear on leaves and stems, weakening the plant. Remove affected growth and keep plants well watered.

Rust Infected plants develop orange-brown pustules on the leaves, become weak, and may die. Avoid using nitrogen-rich fertilizers, remove affected growth, and keep beds free of plant debris. Fungicides can be applied.

Brown rot on fruit This mostly affects damaged fruit, which soften, turn brown, and shrivel up. White pustules may then appear. Protect fruit from bird damage, remove affected fruit, and apply fungicide.

Bolting This refers to plants, often leaf crops, suddenly flowering, after which they soon die, ending the harvest. It is caused by heat or moisture stress. Sow seeds at the recommended time and keep plants moist.

Scorch The leaves of any plant can be damaged by strong wind (*above*) or by hot sunlight, causing dead, brown patches. Choose the ideal place to grow crops, keep them moist, and provide shelter if required.

Common garden weeds

Tansy ragwort This annual weed forms a large rosette of crinkle-edged dark green leaves and produces tall stems of yellow flowers in summer. It seeds very freely, so should be removed before it flowers.

Annual bluegrass This annual type grass grows and flowers quickly, and soon colonizes bare soil. It is easily controlled by hoeing around your plants regularly. Do not allow it to flower and set seeds.

Bindweed This is a rampant, climbing perennial weed that spreads via creeping roots. It will quickly smother crops if not controlled. Do not dig it up, as this will spread the roots—use a systemic weedkiller instead.

Creeping thistle A tough perennial weed, problem plants are most likely on existing vegetable patches. Kill them at root level with a systemic weedkiller. Seedlings can appear on new beds and can be easily hoed off.

Hairy bittercress This annual spreads very rapidly by firing its seeds far and wide from exploding pods. Seedlings flower within a matter of weeks. Hoe them off before they have time to flower, and pull them from pots.

Dandelions A perennial weed, mature plants are mostly found in established yards, where the long taproots need to be pulled from the ground whole. It self-seeds freely, so seedlings can occur anywhere. Hoe them off.

Goosegrass This clinging weed will quickly ramble among your crops and can smother smaller plants. Pull it up by hand before it has the chance to flower and produce its sticky seedpods. Hoe seedlings off.

Groundsel A quick-growing annual weed, it will rapidly colonize any bare earth, as well as containers. It flowers and sets seeds in a matter of weeks, and spreads readily. Pull up mature plants by hand and hoe off seedlings.

Shepherd's purse This annual weed produces long spikes of tiny white flowers that lead to characteristic heart-shaped seed pods. Quick to grow and flower, pull it up before it has time to produce seeds.

Creeping buttercup A perennial, this colorful weed spreads via its creeping roots and can soon weave itself among your crops. Seedlings can be hoed off but treat mature plants with a systemic weedkiller.

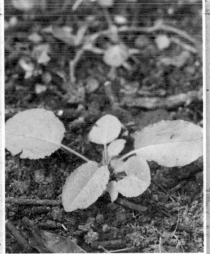

Dock Mature plants of this perennial weed are more common in established yards and have deep roots that are hard to pull up. Treat them with systemic weedkiller. Seedlings can be pulled by hand or hoed off.

Stinging nettle This perennial weed is common in unused urban areas. It forms dense mats of roots that easily regrow, so treat with a systemic weedkiller. Hoe off seedlings or pull by hand, wearing gloves.

Useful resources
Seeds & plants

Gurney's Seed & Nursery Co.
P.O. Box 4178
Greendale, IN 47025-4178
(513) 354-1491
www.gurneys.com

Park Seed Co.
3507 Cokesbury Rd.
Hodges, SC 29653
(800) 845-3369
www.parkseed.com

W. Atlee Burpee & Co.
300 Park Ave.
Warminster, PA 18974
(800) 888-1447
www.burpee.com

**Henry Field's Seed
& Nursery Co.**
P.O. Box 397
Aurora, IN 47001-0397
(513) 354-1495
www.henryfields.com

J.W. Jung Seed Company
335 S. High St.
Randolph, WI 53956
(800) 297-3123
www.jungseed.com

Harris Seeds
355 Paul Road
P.O. Box 24966
Rochester, NY 14624-0966
(800) 544-7938
www.harrisseeds.com

Territorial Seed Company
P.O. Box 158
Cottage Grove, OR 97424
(541) 942-9547
www.territorialseed.com

**The Natural Gardening
Company**
P.O. Box 750776
Petaluma, CA 94975-0776
(707) 766-9303
www.naturalgardening.com

Johnny's Selected Seeds
955 Benton Ave.
Winslow, ME 04901
(877) 564-6697
www.johnnyseeds.com

NESEED
3580 Main St.
Hartford, CT 06120
(800) 825-5477
www.neseed.com

Eden Brothers
34 Old Brevard Rd.
Asheville, NC 28806
(828) 633-6338
www.edenbrothers.com

American Meadows Inc.
223 Avenue D, Suite 30
Williston, VT 05495
(877) 309-7333
www.americanmeadows.com

Mountain Valley Growers
38325 Pepperweed Rd.
Squaw Valley, CA 93675
(559) 338-2775
www.mountainvalleygrowers.com

**Thompson & Morgan®
Seedsmen, Inc.**
P.O. Box 397
Aurora, IN 47001-0397
(800) 274-7333
www.tmseeds.com

Fruit trees, plants & shrubs

Willis Orchard Company
200 McCormick Rd.
Cartersville, GA 30120
(866) 586-6283
www.willisorchards.com

**Stark Bros. Nurseries
& Orchards Co.**
P.O. Box 1800
Louisiana, MO 63353
(800) 325-4180
www.starkbros.com

Cottage Farms Direct
9960 Padgett Switch Rd.
Irvington, AL 36544
(888) 593-3644
www.cottagefarmsdirect.com

Nature Hills Nursery, Inc.
9910 N. 48th St., Suite 200
Omaha, NE 68152
(888) 864-7663
www.naturehills.com

Raintree Nursery
391 Butts Rd.
Morton, WA 98356
(800) 391-8892
www.raintreenursery.com

Gurney's Seed & Nursery Co.
P.O. Box 4178
Greendale, IN 47025 4178
(513) 354-1491
www.gurneys.com

Biological pest control

Buglogical Control Systems, Inc.
P.O. Box 32046
Tucson, AZ 85751-2046
(520) 298-4400
www.buglogical.com

GreenMethods.com
9664 Tanqueray Ct.
Redding, CA 96003
(530) 226-6300
www.greenmethods.com

Gardens Alive!
5100 Schenley Place
Lawrenceburg, IN 47025
(513) 354-1482
www.gardensalive.com

Planet Natural
1612 Gold Ave.
Bozeman, MT 59715
(406) 587-5891
www.planetnatural.com

Arbico Organics
10831 N. Mavinee Dr., Ste. 185
Oro Valley, AZ 85737-9531
(800) 827-2847
www.arbico-organics.com

Sundries & equipment

Gardener's Supply Company
128 Intervale Road
Burlington, VT 05401
(800) 876-5520
www.gardeners.com

Plow and Hearth
Rt. 230 West
Madison, VA 22727
(800) 494-7544
www.plowhearth.com

Garden Tool Company
10 Circle Dr.
Fort Collins, CO 80524
(800) 830-4019
www.gardentoolcompany.com

A. M. Leonard, Inc.
241 Fox Drive
Piqua, OH 45356-0816
(800) 543-8955
www.amleo.com

Tractor Supply Company
200 Powell Place
Brentwood, TN 37027
(877) 718 6750
www.tractorsupply.com

Index

Acknowledgments

Picture credits

The publisher would like to thank the following for their kind permission to reproduce their photographs:

Lucy Claxton (c) Dorling Kindersley 14 FBL; Lucy Claxton (c) Dorling Kindersley 25 CLA; (c) Alan Buckingham 30 FBR; Brian North (c) Dorling Kindersley, Courtesy of RHS Chelsea Flower Show 2009 36 CRB; (c) Alan Buckingham 37 CRA; Peter Anderson (c) Dorling Kindersley, Courtesy of RHS Hampton Court Flower Show 40 CRA; (c) Alan Buckingham 44 FCLB; (c) Jerry Young 55 CRA; Mark Winwood (c) Dorling Kindersley, Courtesy of RHS Wisley 55 FBL; Getty: Reggie Casagrande / Photodisc 57 FCRA; Brian North (c) Dorling Kindersley, Courtesy of RHS Chelsea Flower Show 2011 75 C; Mark Winwood (c) Dorling Kindersley, Courtesy of RHS Wisley 107 FCLA; Joanne Doran (c) Dorling Kindersley, Courtesy of RHS Hampton Court Flower Show 2011 117 C; Peter Anderson (c) Dorling Kindersley, Courtesy of RHS Chelsea Flower Show 2009 157 C; Peter Anderson (c) Dorling Kindersley, Courtesy of RHS Hampton Court Flower Show 183 CRB; Peter Anderson (c) Dorling Kindersley, Courtesy of RHS Hampton Court Flower Show 183 CLB; Peter Anderson (c) Dorling Kindersley, Courtesy of RHS Hampton Court Flower Show 2010 183 CRA; Peter Anderson (c) Dorling Kindersley, Courtesy of RHS Hampton Court Flower Show 201 BL; Joanne Doran (c) Dorling Kindersley, Courtesy of RHS Hampton Court Flower Show 2011 211 CLA; Joanne Doran (c) Dorling Kindersley, Courtesy of RHS Hampton Court Flower Show 2011 221 CRB; Peter Anderson (c) Dorling Kindersley, Courtesy of RHS Hampton Court Flower Show 2010 221 CLA; Lucy Claxton (c) Dorling Kindersley 225 TR; Peter Anderson (c) Dorling Kindersley, Courtesy of RHS Hampton Court Flower Show 2010 229 TR; (c) Alan Buckingham 233 FCLB; (c) Alan Buckingham 233 CRB; (c) Alan Buckingham 234 CRB; (c) Alan Buckingham 244 FCRB; (c) Alan Buckingham 245 FCLB;

Dorling Kindersley would like to thank:

Photography Peter Anderson
Editorial support Esther Ripley and Annalise Evans
Design support Eleanor Bates, Vanessa Hamilton, and Amy Keast
Proofreading Constance Novis
Indexing Vanessa Bird

DK would also like to give special thanks to the following for their kind help in producing this book:
Bruno Lacey and his colleagues at Urban Growth, London, for helping to create and maintain many of the raised beds featured.
Tom Wheatcroft and his colleagues at Capel Manor College, London, for helping to create and maintain many of the projects shown.
Clare Dyson at Pro-Veg Seeds Ltd., Cambridge, for supplying plants.
Faulks and Cox Ltd., Leicestershire, for supplying many of the containers used.